WORLDS

John R. Clayden

Versions of Life
Stories from Counselling

europe books

europe books

www.europebooks.co.uk – info@europebooks.co.uk

ISBN 9791220121125
First edition: March 2022

Distribution for the United Kingdom: **Vine House Distribution ltd**

Printed for Italy by Rotomail Italia
Finito di stampare nel mese di marzo 2022
presso Rotomail Italia S.p.A. - Vignate (MI)

Versions of Life
Stories from Counselling

This book is dedicated to the late Dee Howley.
A good friend, colleague,
and an outstanding counsellor.

This book would not have been possible without the inspiration and dedication of my late colleague Dee Howley and her work with my patients. In that respect I should like to say a sincere thankyou to all the anonymous contributors who, although still working through their own difficulties, gave up their time to put their honest feelings down on paper; both in order to help them better understand themselves and their fellow group members, and in consenting to share their stories to help others find ways of getting help.

I should also like to thank Marialaura Faitini for encouraging me to publish this book, Maria Vitelli for her patience and useful suggestions during its production, and all the other excellent editorial staff at EuropeBooks who have helped to turn my initial concept into a book well worth reading.

Finally, major thanks must go to my wife, Marie, who has been my supporting rock throughout my career both in putting up with the many disruptions to our family life caused by my 40 years work as a GP, and in reading my work and encouraging me to persevere.

No-one is useless in this world who lightens the burdens of another.

Charles Dickens.

Remember the five simple rules to be happy:
"Free your heart from hatred.
Free your mind from worries.
Live simply.
Give more.
Expect less."

Versions of Life – Stories from Counselling

Foreword

A great deal of a general practitioner's time is spent in dealing with psychological and psychiatric disorders. In fact, they are the third most common diagnosis made during consultations. In my long career as a family doctor, I came to understand that many of the troubles bringing people to my door were far more subtle and complex, both in origin and therapeutic needs, than first appeared. Consultations often required huge patience and understanding in order to tease out the 'splinter' in a life that was causing discomfort or preventing healing and resolution.

In trying to find ways to help patients overcome a huge range of troubles from many aspects of life, without overwhelming my abilities to provide a good service for other patients, I eventually was lucky enough to find a counsellor or, more accurately, for her to find me and offer her services. Initially, this was as part of her own training programme and then, as her successes became more obvious, as a welcome part of the practice team.

A psychotherapeutic approach to illness is not exactly new. Among the first dedicated psychotherapeutic clinics was that of the Dutch psychiatrists Van Rentergen and Van Eeden who opened their doors in 1887 with the stated intention that they wished to "cure the body by the mind, aided by impulse of one mind to another." In this country, although the traditions of psychotherapy were accepted and used by psychiatrists from this time, it was not until the late 1960's, when pioneering diploma courses were offered at Keele and Reading Universities, that 'lay' counselling became a fully integrated academic subgroup of psychology. The Standing council for the Advancement of Counselling (now the British Association of Counselling or BAC) was set up in 1971 and by today it has a growing membership of many thousands. During the same time, the value of counselling techniques became more known and accepted both by patients, general practitioners, and psychiatrists, whilst the teaching of counselling techniques in the consultation became a firmly established part of general practice vocational training schemes.

The exact meaning of the term 'counselling' varies somewhat depending upon the manner in which it is approached. For example, the 1984 BAC definition "includes work with individuals and with relationships which may be developmental, crisis support, psychotherapeutic, guiding or problem solving [...] The task of counselling is to give the 'client' an opportunity to explore, discover and clarify ways of living more satisfyingly and resourcefully." On the other hand, Burks and Stefflre, in their 1979 book *Theories of Counselling*, defined counselling as "denoting a professional relationship between a trained counsellor and a client. This relationship is usually person-to-person, although it may sometimes involve more than two people. It is designed to help clients to understand and clarify their views of their life space, and to learn to reach their self-determined goals through meaningful, well-informed choices and, through resolution of problems of an emotional or interpersonal nature."

These older definitions, with some elaboration, still stand the test of time. The professional counsellor Glen

Sheppard, in an article written in 2015 entitled 'What is Counselling?', described the search for a definitive way to describe counselling and concluded that "the definitional challenge is made all the more difficult because of the myriad of uses and activities for which the term counselling applies". Even by 1986 Karasu reported that over 400 models of counselling and psychotherapy were then known, and to this day, there is still no unified approach to the methods or practical techniques used in counselling or, indeed, psychotherapy so that new ideas are constantly being evolved and tested.

This is both a strength and weakness. Continued diversity, due to different educational levels of client and therapist, cultural backgrounds, individual needs and time constraints are bound to occur, and can benefit the needs of a wider population. Counsellors must find an individual and comfortable way of working in order to assist different clients, all with unique problems, in ways which best suit them. The lack of a standard approach, however, often makes it difficult for medical practitioners, with their background in evidence-based science, to understand which method to advise their patients to try, and to accept outside counsellors as having a serious role in the therapeutic programme.

Furthermore, debate about the difference between psychotherapy and counselling has always been waged. Some feel that the two are quite distinct, and others see them as part of the same spectrum of activity where psychotherapy merely involves a deeper, longer process with more disturbed clients. It is often said that therapists and counsellors use similar techniques but different titles depending upon their employing agency. In the community setting, general practitioners, community psychiatric nursing teams, practice nurses, health visitors and other non-professional volunteers have often utilised non-directional 'Rogerian' counselling using empathy, reflection and challenge, with an emphasis on current behaviour and its modification. Psychotherapy, on the other hand, has involved private and NHS psychiatric units and trained clinical psychologists using various specific psychologically based counselling techniques.

Whatever the form it takes, however, counselling has become an increasingly accepted part of our Western social coping mechanisms. Counsellors are progressively involved in areas where we are having problems in adapting to trauma and change. Counselling assistance is now often expected and sought at the major 'cross-roads' of life such as birth, marriage, divorce, seeking employment, facing redundancy, physical and mental trauma, retirement or death and, in 21st century society, we can now see many other forms of counselling relationships where counselling skills are used outside of a more formalised framework. Examples of this include the mentoring aspects of teaching, specific help lines for those with serious health or social problems such as AIDS and drug or alcohol related problems, suicide 'rescue' work by the Samaritans, child abuse helplines, psychosexual problems, the probation service's work in rehabilitation of offenders, and the group support for victims, patients, and their families such as that offered by Alcoholics Anonymous. There is also the support offered to patients and carers by the hospice movement and by religious ministers, hypnotherapists, faith healers, and many others in alternative medicine.

Although psychotropic drugs are still heavily prescribed in the community and hospital setting, patients widely distrust them and worry about their side effects and habituation potential. Many do not wish to take these types of drugs if it can possibly be avoided. The problem is, however, that although ‘talking therapies’ are widely presented, both to the public and the professions, as being the preferable option, for them to be effective in practice requires an exceptional commitment in time, both from the GP and the patient.

As problems of this nature are only one facet of the workload of the doctor in primary care, they must necessarily be the subject of constraints or else other clinically important work will suffer. For this reason, it would seem most sensible and logical to employ trained and experienced counsellors to assist in work with appropriate patients. There are several subjective accounts of the value of counselling in general practice. Past studies have shown a definite reduction in visits to the GP, amounts of psychotropic drugs taken, and psychiatric referrals made by the GP following counselling. Controlled trials to look at counselling have been performed but, in spite of the accepted academic background which now exists, there is still a long way to go before full use is made of counsellors in general practice.

Provision of counselling obviously has a direct cost to primary care and, ultimately, to NHS as a whole. Figures on the financial implications of counselling are not easy to obtain but, from studies we carried out in my own practice, we were able to demonstrate considerable savings, both in prescribed medication and in referral to other NHS facilities and services, even when taking the costs of counselling into consideration.

My own interest in counselling dates back to 1969 and my very first hospital jobs after qualifying as a doctor. I was fortunate enough to be attached to several consultants who had a great belief in the necessity of their junior staff listening carefully to what patients both said and felt rather than just strictly adhering to the usual hospital history and examination protocols. One such consultant, George Craig, a well-loved Bradford obstetrician and gynaecologist, regularly demonstrated by audit that, by listening to patient's fears and properly setting them to rest at the bedside, his patients got better quicker, stayed in hospital for much less time and had a much more positive outlook towards getting back to normal following their surgery.

By the time I entered general practice, I was already hooked on the personal and holistic approach to patient care. As appointment times in the early 1970's were usually five minutes, however, my surgeries soon became renowned for running late! In spite of this, I was convinced that listening and counselling solved more problems than it created and, in the long run, saved time by reducing the number of visits by dis-satisfied patients who, if not listened to, returned repeatedly for further opinions. Later, in 1980, I took over a practice on my own and rapidly instigated a change to ten minutes appointments with twenty minutes allowed for patients who wanted, or regularly appeared to need, more time. I discovered more about counselling through my own postgraduate learning with other enthusiasts who were involved in the work of training new general practitioners. More and more, I came to realise that the solution of many of the day-to-day problems we saw involved the need for the patients themselves, via counselling, to become an active participant in their own healing processes.

When I was later approached by Dee Howley with a view to setting up a proper counselling service for suitable patients, I jumped at the chance, even though there was no government funding and I had to pay her salary entirely from my own pocket. Dee was a warm and gifted counsellor and therapist with whom I was proud to work and who has been sadly missed by us all since her death from ovarian cancer in 2011. From the early beginnings of our co-operation, and with the growth of the practice, we have all come to see our counselling team as essential to the mental health and well-being strategy of the practice – both patients and doctors! We later performed research and audits which confirmed and quantified the value of this service both to the practice, to our patients and, through reduced demand for medication and psychiatric referrals, to other parts of the health service. The structured framework we evolved allowed us to refer the right people for the right kind of counselling. This involved us offering a range of tailored approaches including one to one, crisis sessions, marriage guidance, bereavement and eating disorder counselling.

We also facilitated and offered membership of active patient groups for those who wished to pursue their problems with ongoing peer support. As part of this process, Dee encouraged the group members to write accounts of their troubles and these anonymous accounts form the basis of this book.

John R. Clayden, retired GP.

Introduction

Throughout the course of our lives, most of us will have suffered, at one time or another, with periods of anxiousness, hurt, grief or feeling down. These are the result of normal reactions and interactions with the social world we inhabit. Most of us will manage to cope with these and get our lives 'back on track', often helped by those close to us. However, in a number of people, these feelings may become dominant and lead to more serious self-destructive or awkward behaviour impacting on not only the person themselves, but also on those they come into daily contact with; Their families, loved ones, friends, and colleagues.

As part of a counselling-based general practice approach, and in trying to help those who came to us with emotional difficulties they could not solve themselves, Dee and I evolved various strategies. At this time, very few practices had attached counsellors, so we were gradually discovering the best way to employ her talents as an important adjunct to our own clinical work. As the system developed, many of those we were helping found it useful to join forces in partly self-supporting groups, getting together out of hours, in our practice meeting rooms. The aim of these groups was to try to explore how each person dealt with their own problems and, through this, to support each other in making progress in a manner not unlike the approach used by AA or other similar organisations. The main difference here, however, was that the individual problems encountered by our groups covered a much wider spectrum.

In developing the therapeutic process, and in order to give practical help whilst demonstrating the range of problems we encountered, Dee set the groups various tasks. One of these was to encourage them to 'bare their souls' by externalising their feelings and troubles and writing down as much as they felt able to about just how their lives had come to be in this position at this time. Some chose to write stories, and some poems incorporating their feelings. These individual accounts were then discussed at length, internally, by the group members, but Dee was not trying to use these as part of her psychoanalytical exploration of their individual lives. It was more meant to be a therapeutic tool used to help each group member empathise and feel what it was like to 'walk in their neighbours' shoes'. In this way, she believed it would allow them to see their own problems in a different perspective and develop their own supporting mechanisms.

Discussing the resulting 'versions of their lives' found in this collection of stories was, indeed, helpful to most of those who took part and they agreed that we could use their stories anonymously to help others to consider accepting counselling in the future. The accounts you will read are moving, quirky, and sometimes harrowing reports of the struggles faced by these individuals as they tried to face up to their difficulties. They are, regrettably, not always a good advertisement for the care offered by professionals along the way. The reader may recognise many of the anxieties and pressures described in the following pages as aspects of themselves, or of someone close to them. The troubles we all face as human beings are amazingly similar in many respects: Loss, fear, anger and disappointment are part of everyone's life at one time or another.

Eventually, Dee brought them to me, and we discussed the possibility of incorporating them together as a book for much wider readership. Organising and transcribing these hand-written stories was not an easy task and was further put off by Dee's illness and early death, so it was only after I hung up my stethoscope and retired from practice that I completed and arranged it.

The stories and poems are honest, raw, and sometimes uncomfortable insights into other people's troubled lives. As with their original use in group therapy, we have not attempted to add any clever analysis or even, as counsellors, discuss our own feelings or explanations about them. Instead, the aim is to try and let at least some of their emotions ring a bell with the reader and, possibly, through this to help to move any of their own difficulties or problems forward. There is no end point to each story. Real life is ongoing and new challenges, successes, and failures face us all around every corner of each new day. We do, however, hope that this collection will act as a beacon to those who need encouragement to use counselling and as a challenge for the professionals who will take primary care well into the 21st century and beyond, to try to listen seriously, and respond to the hidden needs of their patients.

Several relevant inspirational thoughts have been included between the individual stories, demonstrating how other, far more well-known, authors have voiced their own feelings about how to deal with problems and the usefulness of supportive input from others.

We hope that anyone reading this book who does feel to be in a difficult hole from which they are struggling to get out might consider obtaining some counselling either by contacting their own primary care medical service, or through a privately recommended, fully trained and supported counselling service.

Some Aims of Counselling

Before reading the accounts of our own group members it may be of value to take a brief look at what modern counselling tries to achieve. Although methodology and delivery may vary, the techniques have in general several common aims which can be summarised as follows.

To increase insight into problems so that decision making is rationalised.

To enable fulfilment of potential and integration of self-conflict.

To increase self-awareness and to become more open to deeper emotions and thoughts.

To increase self-acceptance and to gain a positive attitude towards 'self'.

To encourage involvement in solving problems by working them through with the client.

To teach awareness of psychological techniques, and by this, to improve ability to cope and to manage other behavioural difficulties.

To assist in managing change in areas of cognitive, behavioural and system (e.g., family, workplace) behaviour.

To act therapeutically in helping to get rid of destructive behaviour patterns in various life situations.

To empower the individual so they can confront areas of inequality and unhappiness in their lives.

To assist with resolution of previous problems and the coming to terms with results of previous damaging or unproductive behaviours.

The Castle Keep

It's not often one is asked to write about oneself. Is it even possible to do this without bias? Answering someone else's questions is one thing, but me, delving inside and trying to come up with who and what I am – well that's quite a challenge! What of discretion? What do you leave out? Do people really want to know how I was traumatised at the age of six whilst standing in line for the 'nit' nurse? I mean, I could probably write a whole book so, instead, I will address my lack of self-confidence or inadequacy as it is the one part of my personality that is uppermost in my mind right now.

I guess if I had to categorise my hopes, dreams, feelings and philosophy the nearest label I could come up with now would probably be that I have a somewhat pagan set of beliefs. But who needs labels, right? I have suffered all my life from low self-esteem. This led me at a young age to try the mainstream religions which I'm afraid I found limiting and wanting. Perhaps it's just me, but after the first flush of novelty, I found I wasn't reacting well to being penned in, herded, or being told what to think. Don't get me wrong, I'm not being judgmental, there's nothing wrong with people who join a particular religious club, just the one's I met. After all, we are all individuals – at least, that's what most people would say.

So, I'll concentrate on inadequacy. My own personal variety comes into its own when dealing with other people. I feel as though I have been living in the keep of a castle all my life. People, places and experiences pass by my window so I can see them and touch them, but I never leave the safety of the keep. All this time, however, those I know think I am out there with them. The real beauty of this "keep" is that it changes outwardly depending on who is looking at it. My view remains the same, but my barrier walls lead me to mirror those I am attempting to communicate with. Mimicry is the greatest flattery O.K. So, this way I'll be liked.

Of course, there are all sorts of ways to communicate. My brother once held a conversation in Spanish (a language he doesn't speak) with a Spaniard who spoke nothing else, about how black was really white. No really, he did! On reflection, the hour was late and there was a lot of sangria involved, but communication was definitely made!

I suppose that the ultimate communication, the ultimate connection, comes within relationships. When you first tell someone you love them, the one thing you want to hear back is that they love you too. Then you start worrying about maintaining the love. The fear of losing it is palpable. Personally, my fear is that I'm putting on such a good act that the one to whom my affections are directed doesn't know me at all and has, in fact, been totally fooled, has fallen for the ploy and has succumbed to my machinations! What are they going to do when they realise I am not all, or even any of the things they think I am? They absorb the image that I have manufactured to their needs, and the love that is made manifest. The feelings they might have for me I cannot absorb. They merely bounce off the surface. Why? Because they do not know the real me! They are responding to the image I have shown them.

Why do I do this? Or should I say, why did I used to do this? It was because of my feelings of inadequacy and my belief that no-one could possibly love the real me. A favourite line was "I love you, but you deserve better that me." This immediately diminished their opinion.

"What do you mean better than you?" They would say. So I would turn it into a joke: "You know, someone with a great job, or a beautiful body, or a credit-card that doesn't set off that awful bleeping sound!" Of course, people soon got fed up with my constant pleading for reassurance. I suffered so many failed relationships. Why? Because they were entered into under a disguise, I was waiting for someone to see beneath the camouflage, yet always afraid that someone might because it's a mess down there!

I have to come to terms with myself first. I'm fed up with the disguises. I've had enough of pretence and mimicry. When I change my persona for what I see as someone else's benefit, I am living in fear. Fear of being unacceptable and thus rejected.

Wow! This is getting heavy. But you know what? I finally managed to put love in place of fear, not love for someone else. Love for myself. Does that sound conceited and selfish? – See me squirm! I have begun to realise something. The list of people I love shouldn't be limited and the person on top of the list should be me!

There is a rule though: Behaving in a loving way doesn't necessarily mean letting people do whatever they want. For instance, I love my cat, but he's young and inexperienced, and I can't let him chew through that electric cable even though he's having a great time. What I'm trying to say is; Because something is perceived as good doesn't necessarily mean it is, and now that I have reached the period in my life where I can finally start to work out who I am, I can make those judgments for myself and hopefully actually believe them:

I don't have to be intelligent.
I don't have to be thin.
I don't have to be rich.
I don't have to be popular.
I don't have to be beautiful.

I'm just sorry this took so long! There is of course nothing wrong with any of these things but they are all transient, and one or all cannot, by themselves, bring happiness. All I have to do is love. First myself, then I can see and judge from a solid, reliable standpoint.

If I can remember that I am myself, and answerable only to my own conscience, I ought to be able to put myself in a place where no-one could ever hurt me again, and where it would no longer be necessary for me to hurt anyone ever again; But the very effort negates the point. Sometimes it's the easiest, most natural states of mind that are the hardest to achieve.

The last time I saw my psychiatrist, having gone into colourful detail about my latest inadequacies feeling desperate and shaky, I said, "I don't know what to do!"

"Persevere", was his reply.

'Persevere, persevere', I came away with the word ringing in my ears, 'persevere', you know when you repeat the simplest of words over and over again, it becomes just a sound with its original meaning lost? 'Persevere, persevere', all I was getting was an image of a middle-aged male hairdresser who's never been close to either Vidal Sassoon or Barbara Streisand, but with the ability to steer a conversation around much less interesting topics than your holiday plans, whilst mincing to and fro between customers, a touch here, a quip there 'persevere', yes, okay, 'persevere'…I've got it already!

Perseverance, it has to be said, is not my strong point. I'm more of a 'road to Damascus' sudden flash of inspiration type. There are however no guarantees of success in anything. If there were, we might as well be puppets on a toy stage, a bit like an aging Hollywood actress who's had so many face-lifts she looks permanently startled!

I have striven to know who I am. But who I am changes constantly, and it can be difficult not to let certain things contaminate your mind. Although, it must be said, this can only happen if you let it, if you accept it inside. Of course, 'No man is an island' and all that, but the only person really responsible for your state of mind is you. Nor can you expect any sympathy; No-one can instinctively know you are suffering. Who can see your state of mind? Can you put a bandage on it for all to see?

I would like to achieve self-knowledge and acceptance, even love, all at once, but if it were that easy it probably wouldn't be worth having and we'd have to find a planet for all the psychologists to go! So, it's a question of predetermining goals. We all have them, but isn't it the way we strive to achieve them that makes the difference? Let's face it, most of our time is spent on the journey, rarely do we land in the state we always dreamed about and, if on occasion we do, we soon realise there's something else we could do with; Another journey to another goal. The one thing I can comfort myself with is this journey, that is my life, is still in motion so there's still somewhere to go. I can only strive to be true to myself and my loved ones and above all to keep learning. Difficulties and problems are all opportunities to learn something. The smallest of achievements is a triumph, and other people's bad behaviour diminishes them not me.

I have to rely on myself to achieve my goals, it doesn't work if I transfer that responsibility onto someone else, and my first goal is self-esteem; To love myself. Well, I'm getting there, but I have learned to love my life and it is this that will teach me how to love myself. Why did I lock myself in the keep, use disguises, masks and psychological mirrors? Because I was skimming the surface, bouncing off other peoples' realities never facing the basic reality and thus the responsibility of my own existence. I was hiding and not really communicating at all. If I love myself, I have no need to communicate anything but the truth. Does that make me weak? On the contrary, it should make me strong. So I love the journey that is life, and I am learning to love myself.

Would I like to be intelligent? Sure I would, but what are my criteria for comparison?

Would I like to be thin? Of course, but I'd be the only woman in my family that was, so I don't really rate my chances.

Would I like to be rich? Well yes, actually I've actually been there and experienced that one, and I chose to leave it all behind. It's not all it's cracked up to be and it certainly didn't bring me happiness!

Would I like to be popular? This one is a given. The more I learn to love myself, the more popular I am.

Would I like to be beautiful? In a way we all are, aren't we? We are all made from the same stuff, you, me, everything else on the planet, and I am sometimes quite overwhelmed at how beautiful the world is!

It's taken me a long time to learn this fundamental truth. I'm in my fifties now and the freedom and wisdom that goes with that comes in handy, so what if I wake up one morning, have an overwhelming urge to wear beige, have a tight perm and a strong hankering for a lavender bag?

Respect yourself, the rest should follow.

The Rule of the Last Inch

Now listen to the rule of the last inch. The job is almost finished, the goal almost attained, everything possible seems to have been achieved, every difficulty overcome – and yet the quality is just not there. The work needs more finish, perhaps further research. In that moment of weariness and self-satisfaction, the temptation is greatest to give up, not to strive for the peak of quality. That's the realm of the last inch – here the work is very, very complex but it's also particularly valuable because it's done with the most perfect means. The rule of the last inch is simply this – not to leave it undone. And not to put it off – because otherwise your mind loses touch with that realm. And not to mind how much time you spend on it, because the aim is not to finish the job quickly but to reach perfection.

Alexander Solzhenitsyn,
The First Circle.

One Day at a Time

The events that changed my life happened over two years ago, when I was 38 years old. I was a chronic alcoholic though I didn't really know that at the time and was caught in a vicious circle: Absolutely desperate to stop drinking but unable to do so. I was sick and tired of drinking. I wasn't able to function, or even sleep, without taking a drink (so I thought).

I'm an only child and was brought up by my parents in a strict Roman Catholic household. My father is a quiet man; My mother's incredibly domineering (though you'd never tell to look at her!). Other than that, I had a generally contented childhood, happy family holidays, plenty of friends. I did have terrible insecurity fears and wouldn't let my mother out of my sight. Starting school and leaving my mother for the first time was overwhelming and, throughout my life, I have felt unsure of myself in many situations. As a child, I played piano and was forced to sing by my mother which I hated! As a teenager, I went to an all-girl convent grammar school. I was generally well behaved and obedient. Looking back now, I quite enjoyed my school years. This was followed by college, close to home, where I obtained a degree. I've been working ever since and have built a good career. Initially, I didn't leave home to go to college, as my mother didn't want me to. There are very many things I didn't do or pursue because my mother didn't want me to!

I can't remember having my first drink, though I do know I soon liked it. I would have been about seventeen but didn't really drink much until I was at college. As I had been indoctrinated to not do anything wrong, in those days I didn't drink and drive, didn't smoke cigarettes and never got drunk.

I met my husband in my early twenties and we've been together ever since in a very happy and stable relationship... except, inevitably, in my later drinking years.

My life moved on, happy at home and at work, where I was doing well and promoted several times. I found I liked to have a drink to relax. More and more, I would try to make sure I didn't have to drive so I could have a drink. I used to think the drink made me funnier, wittier and definitely better looking! Over something like fifteen years, I just kept increasing the amounts I drank with seemingly no side effects... until, very gradually, my world began to close in on me. It was as if there were grey net curtains drawn around my whole life. Everything was wrong, and none of it was my fault!

Whether there was a particular moment or event that pushed me from being a heavy drinker to an alcoholic I don't know. It could have been the decline in health and death of my father-in-law of whom I was very fond, or the continual pressure from my mother to conform (to living in a certain type of house, having 2.2 children, wearing particular clothes, etc.) Or, more likely, it's none of these things, just the way I am. The way I react when I have a drink. After all, I'm sure many people have mothers like mine, but they aren't all alcoholics!

Eventually, I wasn't able to start the day without a drink. It kept the shakes at bay and calmed me down. I couldn't brush my teeth without throwing up. Then I would somehow get through the working day, driving myself to and from work. I'd get home and drink more until I passed out and, it's hard to believe, but then things still became progressively worse. Housework had gone out of the window, done in an occasional blitz. Cooking was a thing of the past, just takeaways and ready meals when I could face food. I couldn't even follow a recipe, let alone have the energy to cook. My husband had to fend for himself. We passed like strangers. I was totally exhausted mentally and physically, and on top of this was smuggling bottles into the house, hiding them all over the place.

Everything seemed to slow down. I would spend hour upon hour, drunk, thinking about what good deeds I would do next (help a friend, do some house painting, some gardening...), or what I would say to people who mattered to me (tell them how much I loved them etc.) I lived in a dream world where nothing came to reality, as all that would happen was that I would eventually pass out. Sleep was a thing of the past. I was usually comatose through drink.

Then there were blackouts. I thought this was when someone was flat out on the floor, unconscious (which I was on several occasions), but no. It is the way in which, when drunk, you can function normally, walk around, have conversations, and then can't remember a single thing about it.

Some of the worst times for me have been the memory loss, not remembering a thing from the night or day before where I had been, who I had spoken to, what I had done. All of that hurt the one who was closest to me, my husband. The physical effects, too, were getting worse, the retching, the pains, bloodshot eyes.

I was so frightened of everything, even answering the phone, going to the door, or saying hello to the milkman became hard. I became introverted and paranoid. Yet throughout this time, I managed to hold on to my job, my driving licence, my home.

I was so desperate to stop drinking but too afraid to admit I had a problem, too ashamed to tell anyone, too frightened to seek any sort of help. My husband had gone past the stage of being angry and disgusted with me, cleaning up after me, making excuses for me. God knows why he stayed with me, but he did. He was kind and caring, and fondly encouraged me not to have a drink each day... but by lunchtime I had always succumbed. Nothing I did, and nothing he did, could stop me from drinking. There was no way out. I was a complete wreck, physically and mentally. I didn't want to live, and I didn't want to die. I was caught in limbo.

I would stare at the phone, with the number of the Samaritans by my side, but just could not pick it up.

One Sunday, some friends came round for lunch... of course, no lunch was prepared. I was a mess, coming round from a drinking binge. My husband no longer covered up for me. My friend asked me if I really wanted help. She said she truly wanted to help and she would ring if I was too afraid to.

She rang the Alcoholics Anonymous (AA) help line for me. She spoke to the man at AA for some time, and then passed him over to me. He asked me if I really wanted to stop drinking. If I did, I should get to an AA meeting. The next one was in two days-time. He would arrange for someone to take me if I wanted (I didn't). My friend then phoned the emergency doctor who gave us some medication to calm me down and help with the DT's.

I was feeling so scared, very anxious, and so frightened of what may happen. Terrified of not being able to sleep (I'd always had a drink before going to bed) I sat upright most of that night. The DT's ebbed away, and two days passed without me having a drink. (This was not unusual. I would sometimes go a few days without a drink after a binge).

My husband drove me to the AA meeting, and I arrived one minute late. I sat at the seat near the door (a quick exit?), and someone got me a cup of tea. They all looked fine, well turned out 'normal' people... not a bunch of winos rolling around the place (well, I didn't know what to expect!). They asked my name and said, 'stick with us and you'll be alright'! Wow! They actually believed that I would be OK. The next hour passed, and I listened to what everyone had to say, I identified with their experiences, the way they felt physically and emotionally. It was the first time I'd ever heard anyone talk like that or speak of the same feelings as mine, so openly.

At AA, I was also told I have a disease, that it was a progressive disease and that it could be fatal – but I had a chance to stop it in its tracks. I hadn't known what to expect from AA. I thought there would be strict rules to follow, special drinks or tablets to take. I also imagined there would be a doctor present, but none of this was the case. I was simply told to 'not pick up the first drink' and to get to as many AA meetings as I could. I left that first meeting with a tiny glimmer of hope. 'Keep coming back' was what I was told, and that's what I did.

A few nights later, I returned for another meeting, and people had remembered my name and seemed genuinely glad to see me back. I identified with everyone, poor, rich, jobless, professionals, old, young, male, female, people from various religions... the common factor was that we'd all been to the same place in our heads, no matter what sort of drinker we were, either out socialising in pubs or secretly at home.

AA was a homecoming for me. One big factor that helped was that no-one was judgmental. They didn't much care what had happened in my past and weren't the slightest bit interested in my drinking escapades – they just wanted me to put the drink down and start to recover, to gain a bit of peace of mind just as they had.

At this time, I also went to the doctor, poured out what had happened and had a few days off sick to calm down and have some time to myself. I was on the 'calming' tablets for less than one week and glad to come off them. Again, my doctor was, to my surprise, very supportive, and not in any way critical of my failings.

It took me some time to realise that it is the very first drink that did the damage – not the tenth or twentieth!

After that first drink came that nice mellow feeling encouraging me to follow it up by drink number two, then three, four... and then all bets are off! In other words, my state of mind dangerously 'changed' after I took just one drink.

Another big help for me was being taught to live 'in the day'. Basically, it was easier to try not to have a drink for just 24 hours, whereas the thought of facing a lifetime without drink was initially unbearable. In the first few days, it was better for me to take it 'an hour at a time', then the hours went on and became a day. Looking back to when I was drinking, I would often say to myself 'I'll never drink again'. Since coming to AA, I have never said that. I try to live in the day. The past can't be changed, and I don't dwell on what might have been. The future is unknown; I could get run over by a bus tomorrow, so I try to focus on what is important to make today as good as it can be.

Physically, I recovered very quickly, within a matter of weeks. Being able to sleep solidly for the whole night and actually wake refreshed was great. I could laugh again (one of my work colleagues was amazed when I had a really good laugh at work), it's a great tonic.

I started to look at the twelve steps of the AA programme, and I got a sponsor (another member of AA) to help me through the steps. It dawned on me that it wasn't just a matter of putting the drink down. I had to sort my head out. Sobriety comes with time, not in the instant of stopping drinking.

I've no idea whether any of the events in my upbringing and background played a part in my alcoholism. I suspect they did, but I'm so pleased with my recovery that I have no desire to upset the applecart by looking back, not yet anyway. For me, the best therapy is to look forward to a better future that I can actively create myself rather than dwell on the unchangeable past.

Today's been a good day, as was yesterday and the day before that. In fact, every single day since my friend made those phone calls over two years ago has been good... on a daily basis, I haven't picked up a drink. My worst day sober in these two years is nowhere near as bad as my best day drunk.

I'm so grateful to my friend, to my husband, to my doctor but most of all to Alcoholics Anonymous. AA principles form the backbone of my day, and without a doubt AA has given me my life back. I feel I'm much more open and friendly now, and that pays off in all sorts of ways, not least that I've re-built relationships and can move forward and tackle whatever hurdles come my way.

Acceptance of my drinking problem was a major factor in my stopping drinking, and now I find acceptance the key to many problems, not just drinking. I've had to tackle various events since I stopped drinking, such as family illness, and I've faced them square on without being muddled in drink. I'm constantly changing. Things don't stay the same: Life, events and friends move on, and I move on too.

Now that I'm a recovering alcoholic I see myself as an ordinary woman who leads a normal life and enjoys the simple things, able to clean my house, cook a meal for my husband, enjoy the garden, be a reliable wife and friend, and live with a bit of dignity.

The AA steps helped me to face myself for what I am and admit my defects and all. They then helped me to clear out the damage I had done to others and eventually to make true and sincere amends to those I had hurt. I now have strength in my weakness – that I know and admit that I am an alcoholic, and I know not to take that first, deadly drink. AA has helped me to live alongside drink – I have had no problems in drinking situations such as celebrations from work etc. The first time I was asked to come to the pub, I spent the whole morning worrying how I could say 'I'll just have a coke' without comment from my colleagues! Of course, no one said a thing! Most people are more interested in finding out what's going on with them than to be bothered about me having, or not having, a drink.

My typical day now involves waking up (feeling grateful that I've not had a drink) and looking at the day ahead and what it holds. Then at night, I look back on the day and think about what happened that perhaps didn't go quite right – I look at my part in it and how that could be better in future. I can now recognise when I am going off-track and have the opportunity to pull back. I constantly have AA slogans, such as 'Keep It Simple' or 'Live and Let Live' – in my head. These have helped me through many tricky situations.

Never in my wildest dreams, when I walked through the door of AA, did I think I could have the contented non-drinking life I have now. At best, I thought I might be able to put the drink down for a while. At worst, well it could not have got much worse as my life had ground to a halt. Instead, I found myself free from the compulsion to drink and with a plan for daily living that certainly works for me and helps me lead a full and wholesome life.

My emotions are now genuine and true. In my drinking days, I was always crying, usually false tears. Now I have more sensitivity to other people and can recognize and face my fears and insecurities, jealousies, and disappointments. Right now, I don't have any great dreams for the future. I'd like to continue with my career and, perhaps one day, I might get a dog, but I'm generally happy with my lot. I've gained independence, I am at last honest with myself, and I am comfortable and happy in my own company.

Most importantly, on a daily basis, I don't pick up a drink. The future is bright but, fundamental to it all, I continue to go follow the AA way of life, go to regular AA meetings, and see what I can do to help other alcoholics.

I would say to anyone, if you have a problem with drink and really want help, just ring the AA helpline now. Don't wait. Don't put it off.

Alcoholics Anonymous: 8009177650
https:wwwalcoholics-anonymous.org.uk
help@aamail.org

Take thy needle my child, and work at your pattern, it will come out a rose by and by.

Life is like that; one stitch at a time, taken patiently, and the pattern will come out all right, like the embroidery.

O.W. Holmes.

A Black Hole

I am a 51-year-old male, married for 27 years with two children aged 25 and 23. Since I married, I have always tried to do the best I could for my family and myself. I worked very long hours, studied, and tried to progress in my job. I mostly achieved this, not without cost in terms of time with my young family and loss of personal free time, and I eventually became general manager of a large industrial manufacturer. At this point, I was thirty-two. I had got there by a combination of hard work, perseverance, and a few lucky breaks.

I believe that I am fairly easy-going, fair minded and responsive to other people's needs. Others may not think this at times, but I am sure that if they thought deeply enough about it, they would see it. I am not a loner but, having said that, I feel more comfortable if I am only reliant on my own resources. I do not like to accept help. Not because I am unappreciative or ungrateful, but possibly because I am rather wary of other motives. I don't think that this attitude is in my nature but has come about through my trust being abused in the past.

I tend to think a great deal about most things, perhaps a little too deeply. This can lead to my worrying about things unnecessarily. I sometimes think that if I didn't have anything to worry about I would invent something, but nevertheless I can usually cope with this. Eventually, I realise what I am doing and stop doing it. I read a great deal, sometimes because I have to learn something, but more often to stimulate my imagination. I tend to read science fiction novels for this reason.

I would like to think that I am very ambitious, but the things I have done and said do not really support this. I think that perhaps if I had been prepared to settle for being content with my lot, at some point, things might have been different.

My upbringing during the fifties and sixties was in the main very happy. My parents, like many at that time, didn't have much but were not desperately poor. I grew up on a council estate until I was sixteen years old, when we bought a new house. By this time, I had made all my friends and I had transport, so I never really became involved with the life of the village. When I left school, at sixteen, the friends I had had since being five seemed to just fade away. There was nothing particularly bad or nasty about this. We just drifted apart and lost touch. Maybe because we went into different things and all found new friends and interests, or because the middle sixties was such a time of change and everything and everyone got swept along with it. Anyway, I don't regret it. I never found it hard to make new friends and things were, for the most part, fine. We had some good and a few not so good times and never got into too much trouble. I suppose I was fairly normal, had girlfriends, good mates and in general was fairly normal, for that period.

Then I started work. I feel that is when I started to be unhappy, not because I am lazy or think that the world owes me a living, but because I hated what I was doing. I knew almost immediately that I did not want to be an apprentice engineer. I bore very easily and much of the work was boring. I tried to quit once but it caused such family arguments that I gave in and stayed at it. I was hampered in that I had not got a clue what I did want to do, and I had been brought up to 'not look above my station.' What nonsense! This, I believe, is where things started to go wrong. I drifted along through this period. Having said that, I did gain qualifications in my field, I did learn to do the job well and I gained several promotions. But I did not gain much satisfaction.

This situation continued until I got married. I had reached the position of shift foreman and realised that it was as far as I was going with that company. I was extremely unhappy and left the company for a slight promotion. My new firm was not good to work for, but at least I didn't feel as low. After a year, I was asked back to my old firm with the promotions I would never otherwise have got. Three years later, I was made redundant and got the job as general manager at a company in Wales, where I stayed for two and a half years. Through all this period I was fairly happy, though very busy and highly stressed. But I coped.

The next sixteen years were taken up as partner in a family run manufacturing firm. I left the job in Wales to do this. Unfortunately, my partner was older and we did not share the same expectations in life. I let him dominate me too much and things never really developed into what I would have liked. I thought at first that I could change things when he retired but the retirement kept being put off and so never happened. Had I put my foot down and refused to accept this, maybe things would have worked out differently, but I didn't and so just drifted on in a sort of comfortable complacency. This was where my present problems started. I know this now. Eventually, trade got very bad, and I decided it must stop before we got into debt. Perhaps it was the excuse to get out. This time, I stuck to my guns. But closing down, selling the machinery and having to let the workforce go took its toll. A year later, I have still not properly recovered.

After it was all over, I took a holiday. I was physically and mentally exhausted and this was to be my recovery time. I obviously didn't realise how far things had gone. It actually made it worse. I had difficulty sleeping, could not concentrate and couldn't make even simple decisions. This felt so unlike me, and I could not cope with these feelings. I didn't want to seek help. It felt like weakness, giving in, losing control. I felt helpless and completely unable to affect my own future. At one point I couldn't even see a future. I felt like I was in a black hole. It was getting to the point where I would be overwhelmed by these feelings. Eventually, things got so bad that I had to get help. I saw my GP who at first wanted to prescribe some drugs. I didn't want this and the alternative he offered was counselling. This did help me to understand what was happening to me and, although I did need some drugs eventually, I believe that the main help came from just talking about it.

I now spend a couple of hours a week in a support group, and this is now the only chance I have to discuss things with people who have similar problems. Every week, something different crops up and this makes me look at my own problems from a different angle. Sometimes it is quite traumatic, others it is very positive and forward-looking. I see the group as a place where I don't have to keep up a pretence, where I first admitted to myself that the answers to my problems could only come from myself and not some magical person who could press a button and make things 'normal'. It has also made me look at what I consider normal. Now, when I think about it, it seems to me that 'normal' doesn't exist. We all have our own version of normal. I just want to be me now, so I have to find out what 'me' is. Maybe I will never know, but I try. It still does matter to me, perhaps as much as ever, but it is not something that is going to stop me trying anymore. I believe that the group has helped me to get to this position.

Following counselling help I have begun to talk to my wife, more than I ever did, about things that matter and not just money and house repairs. This must have affected her more than I can imagine, but she never let it show. That has helped. I recently asked her if she thought I had improved over the last month or so. Her answer was that I acted differently than I had. I asked if I appeared to be more normal? She asked me what 'normal' was? So now I am looking for a normal that suits me.

I now understand that it took a long time to get to the state that I was in and don't expect to get out of it overnight. I used to feel guilty about that but don't anymore. I don't think I will ever look at things in the same way that I did before all this happened. I visualise my problem as a big hole that I was slipping into. That hole will never disappear, just be more or less far away. I think that knowing it is there will help me avoid it. That's just my way of seeing it, but it works for me.

The future is now looking much brighter than I could ever have imagined. I am soon to set up in partnership on a venture that I think I will enjoy. It will be hard, but I don't mind. My new partner is aware of the position (as regards my illness) and does not see it as a problem, so the plans are going ahead. Sometimes I feel very down and apprehensive about the new venture. I tell myself that it is understandable and things will get better. I try to look at things in a more positive way than I did before. It doesn't always work but I try. Also, I have started to realise that there is so much help out there for most things. It's just a matter of looking for it and asking. Something I had stopped doing. I have learned to stop making assumptions about people, organisations and government agencies. Sometimes they are as bad as you imagine but often they are not, and can be of real help.

For all that has happened to me in the last year, and all that is still to come, I do feel more like I did when I was in my twenties and thirties. I know it will not be same; I know more now than I did then so I won't do things from ignorance (as much). I will certainly never be the same again. The hopeless, lost feeling can never be forgotten, but now I am aware that it is there it can be watched for and dealt with.

I do not yet feel confident enough to suggest anyone could learn from what has happened to me. Everyone needs to do their own learning in their own way, and in their own time. I would suggest that the key is to let people help. It is so easy to think that nobody knows what you are going through, but perhaps you are not as different or weak as you think.

Wondering

I lie here and wonder; is this me?
Is this me trapped and yearning to be free?
The moon and stars look so serene.
So contrary to the world my eyes have seen.
I've tried to reach them… but sadly in vain,
Some people will laugh but I'm not insane.
I just have a dream, a different goal
Of a place where there's freedom
Within my own soul.
But what is freedom, and where is it found?
Just where is this place where my soul is bound?
It could be here where I live every day.
Where I was raised, where the kids still play,
Just as I did, in those innocent days,
Before I had entered life's endless maze.
But there is a way out, or so I believe.
Sometimes it's hard for me to perceive.
Perhaps if I put my dreams to good use.
They may set me free and untie my noose.
The answer I know is in my own mind,
Although my mistakes I cannot rewind.
I must look forward, try to see far ahead.
Relish the future, forget all the dread.
A positive mind is a gift from within,
And the tale of my dreams I can never begin.
To tell you of the place that I so much yearn,
A place of such beauty of which I long to learn
But I suppose this place, if I give it some thought
Is a place where the beauty is perceived and not taught.
So I'll try and focus on my visions, so bright.
And I won't allow my aspirations to be obscured by the night

And when my path finally becomes clear,
I'll begin my crusade,
My new life will start, and my old one just fade.

Richard Clay

Unwrapping Parcels

I was a woman in my early forties when I realised that there was little else I could do to make my home life even more miserable than it had become. My personality changed daily, even hourly, ranging from screaming tantrums to the depths of despair followed by guilt and, more often than not, confusion at my own behaviour. At times I wondered just how many people inhabited my head!

It seemed perfectly clear to me, and my only other female confidant, that it must be hormonal. I was around 'that age' wasn't I? I chose to ignore or was unable to acknowledge any other emotional factors and baggage to which I was subject at that time and much of which I had carried around for many years. This did not seem to have any relevance to my present state of mind. I decided that my trouble was most certainly due to my hormones.

I didn't have a regular doctor. I felt it hardly mattered but, somehow, I managed to arrange a doctor's appointment amid my frantic schedule of work and mad dashes around the country to visit my husband. He was at home on the day of the appointment, and I made him attend with me to testify to my erratic and unacceptable behaviour. I had no intention of being passed off as weepy woman in search of sympathy and tranquillizers. I hadn't got time for nonsense. I needed action. I believed that what I needed was a hysterectomy at the very least! That would solve the problem surely?

I can clearly remember the consultation with the doctor. Whilst I spoke to her, tears were spilling down my face. I was furious. I can remember pointing to them and yelling at her; “Look, will you, look. This is nothing to do with me! What is going on? Why are my bloody eyes leaking? I’m not doing it!” My husband sat resignedly in the corner. Nothing would have surprised him. “I need a hysterectomy”. I wailed, “Get rid of the lot. I can’t stand this. I’m not in control!”

My outburst surprised the doctor and my self-diagnosis clearly amused her, as she was unable to stifle a giggle. She gently and plainly explained to me why offering up a large portion of my internal organs was unlikely to help. She did take blood to test my hormone levels but then added that she would like me to see the resident counsellor and would make an appointment. I took this news much as I would have taken an offer for a cup of tea. It seemed reasonable. What did I care if people thought I was not hormonal but ‘nuts’? I’d go anywhere or see anyone if I could only get some quality back into my life.

Things moved so quickly I didn’t have time to consider what counselling meant. Within two weeks, I was offered a morning slot with the practice counsellor. I did wonder briefly as I drove to the surgery to see her for the first time, what it was all about. But really it was just another appointment in a busy day. I cannot remember a thing about that first meeting, and it is so very hard to look back and describe enlightenment as it happens. The best explanation I can offer is that my life was like a huge bowl of vegetable soup that was boiling over and slowly burning. Now I had to take the soup off the boil. I had to identify all the ingredients in the soup. I had to decide which of them were good for me and which were not and then I had to decide which of those remaining ingredients I liked and which I did not. Most importantly, I had to realise that whatever I threw out was my own decision and that the soup should taste much better without ingredients that I didn't really like. I should not feel guilty about leaving out the metaphorical turnip or cabbage. This was not personal, and even if it was supposed to be good for me but I didn't like it in my soup – then that was completely fine.

My counsellor listened. She has continued to listen to my rambling for what now seems like hours, weeks, months and years. During our sessions, she would gently nudge me along on some occasions so that I pulled things out of hiding places in my past and talked them around and around. Each visit was like unwrapping a parcel. Each parcel containing a memory or feeling. Each time I reached the centre there was an unveiling, a light of understanding. I could see how experiences and conditions had bought about these little packages of behaviour.

Sometimes the contents were unpleasant and, on some occasions, they were a deep shock. My counsellor helped me to reason through. At other times the contents were a complete surprise and therefore a shock of a different nature. Sometimes the contents left me speechless. Sometimes I couldn't open the package which left me both disturbed and amazed as I came to realise the power of the psyche. I slowly began to understand that every event, every moment of my life had made me the person I was. I'd had a huge life. I had seen and experienced so many things.

Looking back from where I now stand, I see that once upon a time there was a good person, innocent and naïve. I met someone who took that away and confused me and caused me to create a hard shell of protection. Over the years, the shell grew bigger and harder and actually proved very useful in both life and business. The caring soft person remained inside the shell, but I feared that if it popped out for a second, it would be hurt. However, the huge, armoured carapace with the small soft person inside suddenly found itself in a major department store full of parcels that needed unwrapping. It was going to be a long job.

Six years down the line and I feel very different. My life has changed dramatically because I have now been able to make choices without guilt. If I lose my temper now, I think about it. I ask myself if it was justified and then forget it. In the past, my anger would be all consuming and could be maintained for hours leaving me feeling exhausted and with feelings of hopelessness and depression. I beat myself with a will of iron every day. I did not allow myself breaks or happiness on the grounds that I had never accomplished enough to earn them. No accomplishment was ever to be enough.

One of my most recent achievements is to sit and read and allow dirty dishes to wallow in the sink. 'A small thing' you say? No, not for me! Before, doing the dishes would have led to me washing the floor and the walls, and then cleaning out cupboards ad-infinitum. All this would be after a busy day at work and resulted in me becoming an angry and exhausted woman who finally would collapse into bed. I applied the same tactics to the workplace. Anyone giving me less than 110% was lazy and subject to my displeasure. I led by example and my expectations were high. What a pain in the arse I was! Almost every day I still struggle to a degree with the line between commitment, doing a good job and fanaticism towards my own life and those around me. More often now, however, I can laugh out loud when I stand back and compare how the old and the new me might deal with certain situations.

Recently, I drove many miles to attend an art workshop. I realised en-route that I had perhaps been hasty in booking it. I wasn't really sure what it involved and thought I may spend the whole weekend messing about with nothing constructive to show at the end. I didn't identify that negative slip at the time. By lunchtime the first day I had happily noted interesting ideas from the adjoining gallery and was indulging in placing fabrics and found objects in a haphazard manner all over a backcloth. I suddenly thought, "What are you doing you stupid woman? This is achieving nothing of use to you. You are like a child in playschool."

Another participant must have had similar thoughts and voiced them to her friend. As if it was a voice from inside my own head. The friend replied. "So what? What is stopping you enjoying yourself from taking pleasure just for the sake of it?" How I smiled. I was enjoying myself and I was allowing myself to do it. I banished all my negative thoughts and enjoyed the day.

By mid-day on the next day, however, I began to fidget. Perhaps I could leave early. Get back home organise tea. I might be stuck in traffic it would be late etc. As I glued and sewed, little clouds of anger, peevishness, and discontent floated above my head. I heard someone say, “I don’t care what time I leave, I’m going to stay until I get this finished. If I don’t finish it here, it will never be finished at home.” Again, a small package unwrapped in my mind. Why hurry? Enjoy! The tea will still be there and if I go later the traffic will be less. No one expects you at any particular time. You have a choice. Leave now and arrive home grumpy with unfinished projects feeling that you sacrificed your time to rush back and make a tea that no one expects. Or arrive home smiling, feeling happy and display your finished wares for the amusement of all. Sit down laughing and have a cheese sandwich. The clouds disappeared.

I see the choices each day now. I hope in the years to come I will even stop defining them and simply make the right choices by instinct alone. I could not have come this far without my counsellor or my brilliant husband. The latter has observed the changes and weathered the tantrums and I hope he feels that he now has a calmer wife.

Interestingly, my female confidant, (my mother), has never come to terms with the counselling. When I mention the counsellor’s name, I almost see the sharp intake of breath. My father will have none of it and, on the one occasion I tried to talk to him about his behaviour during my childhood and his own fathers’ behaviour, it was met by such an outburst of panic-stricken rhetoric that I had to leave the house.

I have, and I shall continue to, recommend counselling to all and sundry. I wish it was part of the school curriculum. To be able to speak to a non-judgemental third party, someone who can help you to understand your actions and reactions and those of others toward you. There could be no better qualification to start you off in life.

Where do I go from here? Which parcels of my mind are still to unwrap?

I have been to a few seminars and workshops most a little weird and wonderful, but still always learning. I would like to learn more, but I am not really sure where to turn. I have read books, some good some bad. I have even made some interesting observations in relation to the power of witchcraft and concluded that it has little to do with powders and potions. It is merely an old relation of counselling and self-empowerment.

Now, where did I leave my broomstick?

Everyone carries their parents, an adult and a little boy or girl around in them as aspects of their personality.

It is only when one or the other of them disturbs the healthy balance that analysis and reorganisation are indicated.

Eric Berne,
Games People Play.

******

There are great victories and struggles and noble acts of heroism done every day, in nooks and corners, and in little households, and in men and women's hearts – any one of which might reconcile the sternest man to such a world, and fill him with a hope and belief in it.

Charles Dickens

Changing for the better

I was born in Bolton, Lancashire in 1971. After my Mother gave birth to me, I was sent away to live with my Aunt and Uncle because my natural Mother had no security and was having strained relationships with different men. By the time I reached the age of nearly nine, in 1979, I was placed in the care of Bolton Social Services due to my Aunt stating that she could not cope with me anymore and was unable to offer me the security or help that I needed and hence my next home was to be a foster home. Social Services put me in the classification of a 'problem child'. Although now, when I look back, this was an unfair category to place me in. I was simply emotionally insecure and although I was spoilt in a financial sort of way, my main wants in life were love, affection and security and these had never been shown to me.

In my new foster home, I was physically abused by my foster parent's older son who would continuously hit and punch me when I would go to bed at night. I ran back to my Aunt on two occasions and it was eventually decided by the authorities that I should go into a Children's Home. At the home, I was very happy for almost two years until, eventually, I started being sexually abused by another resident who was aged sixteen. It did not just stop at abuse. I was male raped, something which I will never forget. The scars and memories still appear to me in nightmares, even though this happened almost 20 years ago. I never told anyone about what had happened through fear of disbelief and embarrassment. The Children's Home eventually had to close down due to lack of local authority funds and I was then sent back to live with another perverted Uncle and alcoholic Aunt, even though I pleaded that I did not want to live with them. I was sexually abused by my Uncle and physically abused by my Aunt. I ran away from their house sixteen times and was eventually moved again by Social Services, who told me the next home was my last chance.

This time, I was moved to Chorley in Lancashire with a couple who had two young children. They and Social Services told me that I was not the ideal child that they wanted but, for financial reasons, they were willing to foster me. At first, they appeared to be nice with me, but eventually turned extremely nasty. I was bullied by them both physically and mentally and treated indifferently from their own children. My life was a complete nightmare and one I am still coming to terms with i.e. to try and forget. Again, I was moved to another foster home in Darwen, Lancashire. The new foster parents were nice enough and I was soon getting ready to return to my original Aunt and Uncle who gave me up when I was nine years old.

I returned to Bolton with vengeance on my mind. I was angry, hurt and annoyed about what had happened to me. I had been left physically and mentally disturbed. The first thing I did was visit a doctor to request him to put me on tranquilisers for my anxiety, which he did. I was living life like a zombie with very little money to live on, so I turned to the streets and became a prostitute, dressing as a woman and getting paid for being abused. My only friends at the time were other prostitutes who could understand what I had been through because they had suffered very similar problems throughout their lives and did not prejudge me for the way I was. I was arrested and charged for soliciting on several occasions, which now I obviously regret. Whilst working as a prostitute, I turned to illicit drugs and would often try to end my life, either by slashing my wrists or taking overdoses. I really do not think I was doing this to end my life, I think at the time it was a cry for help, my life as a prostitute and transvestite seemed worthless, which it was now I look back.

At the age of 18, via a chat-line, I met my current partner and found some real security and love. For the first time in my life, I was shown real affection. I then moved out of my Aunt and Uncle's and went to live with him. At first things were fine, but I became violent from mixing tranquillisers with alcohol. I had so much anger built up inside of me that I just wanted to hit out at somebody, and unfortunately, as often is the case, this was my soul mate and partner. I am glad to say I am still with him today, but he did put up with an awful lot of verbal and physical abuse. I really wanted to hurt the people who had damaged me in the past; I did not want to purposely hurt him. One day, he had taken so much physical abuse that he was driven to hit me back. From that day, we did have our arguments but very rarely did they ever result in fist fights. I had learned my lesson. The problem was my mental illness. It was receiving so many diagnoses I never understood what was really wrong with me until the year 2000 when I was admitted to local a psychiatric unit for attempted suicides and self-harm (consisting of me burning my arms with cigarettes and abusing benzodiazepines). The hospital made me feel secure. I was hidden from the outside world and did not have to face anyone if I did not want to. It was a kind of hideaway for me; I did not want to be in the real world. I hated it!

Whilst in hospital, I decided I would rather live my life as a woman and began to dress as one on a full-time basis. I believe now that this was because I was not happy with the way I looked like a man. I felt ugly, fat and grotesque. My behaviour in hospital was chaotic and unreasonable. I was almost refusing the help I was being offered and just feeling pity for myself and being nasty with my partner and my Aunt who would regularly visit me. I was not the real caring, affectionate and listening James that I used to be anymore. I did not appear to care about life or anyone close to me.

Then I decided to escape from England altogether. I thought that the grass would be greener on the other side, and I would be a different person. I was wrong. I ended up spending almost five weeks in a Majorcan hospital on a psychiatric ward and had to be let out by the British Consulate. On return to England, I went into hospital again suffering with depression and personality disorder. Eventually I was well enough to leave the hospital but, just two weeks later, one of my best friends threw herself under a train and I once again cracked up and had to go back in. I eventually came out again and went to my friend's funeral where I had to hold everyone together.

I could not grieve myself, which was another strain on my illness, and the only thing I could think about was running away once more which I did; This time to Fuerteventura. Again, the grass was no greener on the other side. I was soon abusing tablets and alcohol. Eventually, for my own mental state, I returned to

England, but I soon started self-harming again; Both taking overdoses and burning my arms with cigarettes. I was admitted for 72 hours respite care. I was referred to a C.P.N. (Community Psychiatric Nurse) and I was given outpatients appointments, which I now regularly attend, for my medication and a depot injection.

It is now time that I started to believe in myself and allow people to help me instead of rejecting their advice and stop mutilating my arms. My aim in life is to try and put the past behind me. To take my medication as prescribed, appreciate the good things in my life and become a better person. It will take time, but I am sure I will eventually reach my goals. Now, thankfully, I am back with my partner again. I have a supportive general practitioner who referred me for counselling, and I feel much more settled. I know that I am back where I belong which makes me feel even better. I am improving day by day and, with the help from my partner, my C.P.N. and group therapy with my counsellor, I have not burnt my arms for weeks. I want this to be a new chapter in my life. I do have qualities to offer; I am really a nice person who likes to help people, but sometimes I just have really bad depressing days where I can do nothing and let people down. However, I am learning some good coping strategies to overcome these difficulties. I suppose you can say that my life story is 'to be continued', but at last I am truly confident that it is going to be a story with a change for the better.

The Victim

All the emotions
Build up inside,
I try to run,
I try to hide.

I hold it back,
I want to cry,
It hurts inside,
I want to die.

I hate my life,
I live each day,
They will not stop,
Daren’t ask or say.

An Anonymous client aged 14.

The Burning of Leaves

Exiled in Yorkshire, I have been a wife and mother for more than three-quarters of my life. To be anyone else has never crossed my mind. I had known my husband since I was sixteen and we married young. We had four children who over the years grew into mature and confident adults. I was a happy and contented person.

My husband's career moved us several times; From Liverpool to Wigan, then to Bolton and to Yorkshire where we finally settled. As long as we were all together, I didn't ever mind. I told myself that my family was all that mattered in this regard, and I thought we were a good team.

Each time we moved, making new friends and relationships seemed to become more difficult for me. My children seemed to manage well, as children often do. They meet others at school, the local youth club or pubs and nightclubs as they get older and form relationships easily, but I sometimes felt quite isolated within my home and family. Not meeting the children at the school gate meant I didn't meet the mothers who congregate and socialise. I worked full time hours, which didn't leave much time after household jobs, to seriously go out into the neighbourhood and network.

I was that much older too, so I was coming as a fresh face into relationships that were already well established and had a history, while my long-term friends were back in places I had come from. A lot of effort in terms of travel and time was needed to maintain the contact. There was no more 'popping for a chat' type visits. As much as

I loved them, I often envied my kids ability to go out there and have fun. I had been married more than 30 years and my family had flown the nest. There were now grandchildren and life was settled. I had the opportunity to take early retirement from my job as a social worker and in September 1993, I left work after almost 15 years and started looking forward to time for me!

I had so many plans. My husband had spent years climbing the corporate ladder and had no plans to retire early himself, but his work often took him to interesting places, and I would be free now to go with him. This had always been an option before, but my job and family left me little time to do this.

A month after retiring and staying at home, I had been out for the evening and returned home at 9.30. I had left at 7.00 and hadn't taken a key because my husband was there. This was a weekly outing and I always returned around the same time. Never before had I been unable to get back into my house, but this evening the door was firmly locked. I knocked and rang the bell and only then did I realise my husband's car wasn't on the drive. I couldn't believe that I hadn't noticed! Immediately, I was apprehensive. I thought that something must have happened to a family member, my husband had been called and he hadn't been able contact me. I was fearful that it wasn't good news.

However, I still couldn't get into the house, so I walked to my daughter's home, a mile away, knowing that she held a spare key. She drove me back, so fortunately she was with me when I opened the door. I quickly looked for a note to tell me if there was a problem. There wasn't a note as I half expected, but there was an envelope propped up on the hail table. Inside the envelope, there was a letter from my husband telling me that he had left me and wouldn't be returning. No explanation as to why, other than he couldn't live with me anymore.

I felt cold and then hot and there was buzzing in my ears. I could barely see anything as objects jumped in and out of focus. I can remember my daughter shouting my name and crying loudly as the awful news began to sink in. I dropped to my knees, and I felt dazed and disbelieving. I could not comprehend what was going on.

My initial response was that this was some terrible joke. I couldn't spend thirty-six years with someone only to find after all that time that he couldn't live with me. What a bad person I must be if a man will give up everything he has worked for because he couldn't bear to live with me. Why had he never said? Why had he never talked to me? What had I done? It must be my fault! He had felt so bad that he couldn't bear to be here.

My other daughters and my son came as soon as they were called, and the next few hours were spent trying to rationalise the situation. None of us thought about bed. I don't think we would have slept anyway. I was held in a bubble of disbelief, but the worst was to come as the shock and realisation sank in. I can remember running through my house looking for evidence that this was all a dream, only to find that every drawer with his personal stuff in was empty and all his clothes were gone. Nothing was left of the man I had lived all my life with, not even a spare sock! Even his dirty clothes in the wash basket had been removed. It was as though aliens had been into my home and removed my husband and everything he owned, leaving no trace of him ever having been there. I had an awful sense that people would look at me and pity the woman who talked about her husband who had lived with her and who had disappeared. That only they really knew that I was imagining he had even existed. Where was the proof of his existence within my home? There was none.

Everything else was as it had always been. He had taken nothing, only himself from this place and left me devastated and in despair! It was 5th October 1993. My family was as distraught as me. They too had thought that everything in our home was fine. Now, also like me, they were held in pain and disbelief. No contact was made from my husband, and this was before the mobile phone made it hard to hide. So, I had to wait until I could contact him at his place of work. I didn't know where he was.

I phoned his work as early as I could the next morning and I could barely recognise the man I was talking to. He was cold, hostile and gave me no reason to explain what was going on for him. He just wouldn't live with me anymore. Practical issues came up for me. Where was he living and where had he slept the previous night? It had been quite late when he left home. It must have been late because he had done so much before I returned, collecting all his clothes and belongings the way he had done. He told me he had been renting a small house for a couple of months and had waited until the time was right, when I had left the house, to go!

Such planning and I hadn't had a clue. Finally, I understood how other women I had read about had honestly not had any idea that their partner was going to leave them and now it had happened to me, and I had never suspected. In my innocence, I had never seen clues that may or may not have been there.

Time for me after that passed in a blur. The first two weeks I couldn't sleep in my house, so I stayed with one of my girls until I felt I could return home. I couldn't sleep, but I didn't want to get out of bed either. I couldn't be bothered washing myself or doing my hair. My daughter had to remind me so that personal care was done. I functioned on automatic pilot. I had to drag myself round to complete even the simplest task. Time was standing still. I knew that my body and mind were in shock, but I couldn't ever imagine getting through this awful time. I couldn't eat and weight was dropping off me. My family was also suffering, but for the first time in their lives, I felt unable to help them. I couldn't help myself.

It was October, and the change in the season was a problem for me too. Light and colour was changing, and the world felt cold, drab and grey. I felt my pain in such a physical way too.

I itched all over and I scratched until I bled. This lasted for about a week and physically I knew I looked a mess. I had to have doors open despite it being cold as I felt I couldn't breathe, and I would stand at the open door taking massive lungs-full of air as though I would never get enough. Many times, I had a sensation of falling. I felt myself in a corner, my hands on the two walls pressing my back against the solidness of the plaster so that the corner itself couldn't open up and give me the space to fall through, because I knew that if I did fall through, I would never stop falling. I would fall so far that I wouldn't be able to come back.

I likened my situation to bereavement, but felt that for me, an unwanted separation was worse. I had suffered the shock of losing someone without any warning. However, I could take no comfort from the ritual of death and the acceptable mourning period which follows. I had no cards or words of comfort from the community or acquaintances who knew us both. There was no ceremony to mark the end of an old life and the beginning of a new one, however unwanted. My husband hadn't died still loving me!

I couldn't believe this despair would ever end. There was no light at the end of my tunnel. At times, I teetered on the edge of a large hole. Then I would fall into it, and I came to recognise and dread the knowledge that I was going to feel even worse for some time before I would somehow know that I had cautiously climbed up the sides of the hole a little. As bad as the hole was, it somehow felt safe too. People talk about the memories that are evoked by songs and music from the time they were with a particular person and what it brings up for them… But I had been with my husband since 1959, so I couldn't listen to songs from the 60's 70's or 80's without feeling sick and despairing. What a range of music with so many memories to avoid! Christmas and New Year passed, and I was so glad that they had come and gone. These were the times of such happy memories, and I struggled to cope with the unfamiliar situation of being a woman alone.

Survival kicks in when you least expect it and in an unexpected way! I learnt from my children that my husband had someone else and that they had been together for more than a year. He had been having an affair! Amazingly, the relief was enormous. I felt the biggest weight taken from my shoulders. This explained everything for me! It wasn't my fault after all. I wasn't responsible for my marriage break-up. I was one of those women who, when asked, say that they had no idea that their husbands had been having an affair. I knew the other person involved too. She worked with my husband and was younger than our children.

I couldn't believe that my husband had succumbed to this temptation. He had always been so judgmental of others who had done the same thing. The impact this knowledge had on me was massive. For the first time in months, I could lift up my head and feel the warmth of the sun. I felt the first bubble of life come up inside my chest and into my throat. It was the 23rd of April 1994. At last, I could set about raking up and burning the dead leaves of my old life and think about starting again.

I was able to look at where I was financially. Insurances don't pay out for a separation like they do for a death. My only income was the pension I had from my job. My husband had left me everything and taken nothing, but I had no way of funding the cost of my living. There was a mortgage on the house and a loan on my car. I was 52. Who was going to take me on to work for them at my age? I felt old and useless. I had lost three stones in weight, and I felt small and insignificant.

I finally took on three jobs to keep myself. I worked in a small pub at lunchtime leaving at 4.00 pm. I then went to a doctor's practice and worked as a receptionist before leaving after surgery and working for the evening in another pub. I could keep my head above water! Having little time also meant I couldn't ponder on my situation too much!

I felt the first stirring of recovery.

As I adjusted to my new life on my own, I knew that living in the house I had shared with my husband was a difficulty I was in no position to change. I couldn't afford to move, and my house was a perfect size for my new situation on my own. If I couldn't change my home, then a change in me was needed! I knew that if I stayed the same, I would always miss my husband in my life. There would always be a hole where he had been. But if I changed enough, then how could I miss him in that way? He would never have been a part of my new life so no hole could exist for me. I changed everything about myself (well maybe not everything; some things were new, but some were just rearranged). I decided to go back into education.

I completed a one-year certificate course in my chosen subject and then a three-year diploma course. I met and interacted with so many people who I would never have known in my other life. It was wonderful! I changed myself totally. Not only had I done a lot of work on my own emotional well-being, but physically I needed to be different too. I cut and changed the colour of my hair. Losing weight during the early part of my separation became a bit of a bonus because I felt and looked better.

Out went my old wardrobe and in came the new. I had more energy and a much greater interest in life.

Time has passed quickly, and I look back at the eight years that have gone. I have made friends with so many people and I certainly have a varied life. I don't have to do the three jobs I did for so long but work within my chosen field for which all that learning prepared me.

I go on holiday with my sister every year to foreign climes and we have a brilliant time.

Life is great!

So, what have I learned from my experience?

I have learned that I honestly have no problem at all with anyone wanting to change their life, after all, we only get one go at it. But I do believe that we all must take responsibility for our own actions and if any decision I make for myself is going to cause great pain for another, then I must also take some responsibility for the process. Sadly, my ex-husband didn't take care of me when I most needed him and at a time that was probably difficult for him too. Although he made the decision to go, my learning has taught me that he probably suffered a great deal of guilt and remorse too. If he needed to go then, after so very many years together, we surely could have helped each other to ease the passage of our separation.

I have learned never to be complacent about who I am and what I am doing and never accept that things will stay the same just because that's the way they have always been! As much as I love my kids, I will never again lose myself within the safety of that love. I would never want to return to the pain of the early days of my separation. It took me two full years before I could sit in the living room or on the settee I used to share with my husband when we were married. But I have no wish to return to the life that I thought was so happy before. I have learned to make a bonfire of the dead parts of my old life and to look forward to my new life every day.

I have never seen my husband again since he left.

The Burning of Leaves

Now is the time for the burning of leaves.
They go to the fire; the nostril pricks with smoke
Wandering slowly into a weeping mist.
Brittle and blotches, ragged and rotten sheaves!
A flame seizes the smouldering ruin and bites
On stubborn stalks that crackle and resist.

The last hollyhock's fallen tower is dust
All the spices of June are a bitter reek,
All the extravagant riches spent and mean,
All burns! The reddest rose is a ghost;
Sparks whirl up, to expire in the mist: the wild
Fingers of fire are making corruption clean.

Now is the time for stripping the spirit bare,
Time for the burning of days ended and done.
Idle solace of things that have gone before:
Rootless hopes and fruitless desires are there;
Let them go to the fire, with never a look behind.
The world that was ours is a world that is ours no more.

They will come again. The leaf and the flower, to arise
From squalor and rottenness into the old splendour
And magical scents to a wondering memory bring;
The same glory, to shine upon different eyes.
Earth cares for her own ruins, nought for ours,
Nothing is certain, only the certain spring.

Lawrence Binyon, 1942.

The Wheel of Life

I have accumulated a lot of books over the years. They were chosen because of my varied interests. It is possible that some of them could have been on the shelf for twenty years or more. However, as I am getting older, and becoming disgruntled with life; 'Nobody's right only me' and so on, I recently picked up and decided to read one of my old books. I discovered a book I couldn't remember having bought. It was entitled 'How To Discover Past Lives'. So that was my choice. Although I was brought up as a Methodist, I have always believed in reincarnation, which I think was part of the very first known religions.

Years ago, after a difficult birth of my son, born with the aid of forceps, I heard wonderful music I knew lots of musical works by many composers, but this was unfamiliar to me. I didn't want the music to end as I felt so relaxed and happy just listening. But eventually everything faded, in truth I was very ill and so was my son. I was not allowed to see him. My husband went with him into the little chapel at the hospital to be christened. Apparently, he was very badly bruised all over. His head was black, swollen and badly shaped. Oh yes, Pisceans naturally. The stitches I had to have all became septic later, I had to have three salt baths a day. Even as a baby, I was very frail. The doctor gave my parents no hope at all. I was born with bronchitis and a weak heart. I, myself, was christened on the hearth in front of the fire by William Snowdon. My dad said I looked exactly like a skinned rabbit. All I could take was my lips were gently wet with whiskey periodically. I have had a lot of illness during my life. I have suffered a brain haemorrhage and meningitis; I well remember the pain. But I was in a coma for a very long time, for which I have no memories.

Well, thinking back on my shaky start to life and where my life had led, I glanced through the book turning page after page and then decided to read a couple of pages at random. The paragraphs I finally read focused mainly on an ancient wooden door. Carved and painted on the door was the exact image of the tarot card known as 'The Wheel of Fortune'. I was already in bed, so I closed my eyes and started thinking about the door. But, unlike the door in the book, the door I visualised was plain with a gothic arch at the top similar to those you find in a church. I listened to my old clock ticking, at the same time glancing through the breadth of the bungalow where I live to the wall at the back where the clock stood. I noted with pleasure the smell of wood polish and the rag rugs (mats made from strips of cloth remnants) that my mother used to make, and which were now placed all along the floor to the clock. I liked the atmosphere and looked back fondly at the same time smelling a lovely cooking aroma. I passed through the door, and it closed very gently.

I looked around outside, in front of me was an unusual valley. I felt panic and turned back to the door, but I realised it was now locked and I was alone! I wanted to go back because I felt that I knew the place on the other side of the door, and it was so familiar to me. But on each side of me now was a large expanse of grass. I didn't recognise any part of it. Whichever way I went, I could get hopelessly lost. So, I knew I had to go down into the valley. There were trees all the way down and, in the distance, peeping out was the sun. No moon, stars, or colours apart from a blue sky and white clouds. The valley somehow frightened me, but I knew I should have to go down it. But how could I?

Throughout my life, I have always had to do things the hard way. There was never anyone there to help me when I needed someone. I was born under the sign of Pisces, you see, which I feel, put me at a disadvantage. I have always been interested in astrology. For this reason, knowing the problems faced by Pisceans, then if I ever found out that someone was 'trying for a baby', I would tell them to seriously consider the date of conception and, whatever they decided, try to avoid the baby being born under the sign of Pisces.

As a side point, I personally dislike the continual all-pervading talk and discussions regarding sex these days; 'Do it this way – or that', I abhor it! My late husband and I never ever discussed sex or babies, we were happy to give ourselves up to each other and to God's will. To me, this continual emphasis on the sexual part of life ruins the loving aspect of a relationship. I have always thought that although every other animal in the world cannot read, they seem to manage all right without sex education. So why is it so important today? It seems so mechanical, and to teach young children seems daft beyond all reason to me!

In my dream, I returned to the book I had chosen to read that evening. Its narrative referred to the varying seasons but, in spite of this, my view of the valley remained unchanged. I recalled Khalil Gibran's words; 'But if in your thought you must measure time into seasons, let each one encircle all the other seasons and let today embrace the past with remembrance and hope'. Yet in this valley, I saw no change. Ah! If only I could turn back the clock and rhythm so that I could change; Go back and correct past mistakes, change my life! The book continued; ‘It thrills you, and excites you, it reminds you that all is possible in time!’ But, oh no! I knew otherwise, always the hard way for this Piscean. And what is more, how on earth was I going to get down the valley unscathed? Impossible! I could roll down, but some obstacle unseen could maim me, and I was alone. It was very steep and somehow the deeper it went the darker and darker it became. There must have been animals and wildlife around, yet that aspect didn’t worry me as I love all kinds of creatures. I decided to walk very slowly through the seemingly endless valley and, in doing so, all the mistakes I had ever made flooded back to me, there was no escape from them. In spite of this, the journey didn’t seem too bad. I had sips of water from the running stream. Walking slowly, I then started to recall several re-incarnations. The previous lives I had lived.

Firstly, I found myself pleasantly attired in a stately home to entertain guests after dinner. I was engaged as a singer. Initially, I couldn’t decide where to stand. Eventually I stood near to the baby grand piano. The guests were all seated on large blue velvet sofas in a circle and were all in Victorian evening dress.

The next recurring re-incarnation I experienced put me in a huge castle which was very bare. I knew that I was the son of Louis 15th. I was approximately 8 years of age standing in the middle of two guards. In front was a huge door with the large bolts pulled open. I was on a high veranda. I already knew what was going to happen. Several men carrying large spears marched forward. They wore strong metal uniforms with helmets which overlapped their foreheads. They came up the stone steps leading a young boy about my age, and we simply changed places. It never altered, it was always the same.

By now, I was so tired with my walk in the valley that I had to sit down. I was beginning to feel relaxed and sleepy. What I cannot understand is this; I must have fallen asleep, because as I opened my eyes I could see the door of the bungalow was open. The clock was gently chiming. It was exactly as it was when I left! But now I was unafraid, I don't recollect the rest of my journey, but now I could hear familiar voices excitedly awaiting my return! I was back where I had started from!

The wheel had turned full circle and brought me home.

A couple of days before this dream, my mother appeared to me in another dream. It was wonderful to be with her again. We talked of past days. She kept trying to intervene to tell me something, but I was so excited to see her, she couldn't tell me the important news. Eventually, I said; "Oh Mum, you must come again" but she replied, "we are not supposed to".

When I asked her why not, she replied, "I can't discuss it, but I am always with you". I questioned what she meant. She merely said, "I mean what I say!". I felt that was wonderful. It was just what Jesus said, and so I needn't worry about life and death. We talked of loved ones who were no longer with us but eventually I fell asleep in my dream and awoke with that vivid memory.

Whilst I was in the dream valley, I now feel that I was being advised to think things out well in advance.

Returning and reflecting on the dream events of the door and valley, I suddenly realised how wrong I had been to struggle on with people who were not in tune with me. I remembered the saying; 'To thine own self be true and it shall follow as night the day thou cannot then be false to anyone'. I felt that I had wasted valuable time and strength in trying to deal with people who simply didn't care about me. If someone you know irritates you and will continue talking and talking to you on a bus for instance, then change your route and travel on a different bus. Also, if you are deaf exploit it, these people are not worth listening to, avoid them. They drain your energies and are unworthy of your sensitive nature.

That was one lesson I learnt; Jesus said; "Love your enemies", but I think by that he meant we should learn to accept them for who they are as our enemies, even though it is unlikely that they will ever become our friends. People don't change. Another discovery I made was that I could see that though many of the mistakes I had made throughout my life were actually provoked by other people, they also involved me, and I had to accept that there really were two sides to every story. I must learn to 'carry the can' even though they might walk away uncaring! Sometimes, I feel that although I have always kept my word all my life it has never, ever, done me any good at all!

The Hours Between

The hours between sunrise and set
Are not just emptiness or space
But full of memories, yet
Held tight within my heart's embrace.

One might think the time twixt years
Would make opaque the endless fears
Yet memories remain, if rearranged,
Etched beyond repair-
Immovable, unchanged.

Each day the sun, the moon
and life bring forth their endless showers.
The laughter and the tears
That deck those fleeting hours
Passing all too soon

Then suddenly a rainbow may appear
And magically paint the day.
Or a nightingale we hear
To chase the darkest night away.

And so the hours between
Will fill again
The warmth of friends
Will soothe our pain
And make amends.

Muriel Kelly

A Figure to Die For

It would be completely wrong and hypocritical for me to assume that I knew what was going on the minds of all people suffering from what is now political correctly termed as “eating distress”. I would not be so presumptive as to begin to imagine how others have battled and endured such an addictive and destructive illness, but the only way that I can perhaps show some empathy is by writing my own account of the events that either caused or contributed to my own anorexia. The food element of any eating disorder is, in my opinion, purely a symptom and not a cause of an underlying illness or emotional problem. It is the negative way in which we are conveying our feelings or crying out for help or attention and happen to use food to do it. I could just as easily have become a compulsive eater, an alcoholic or a drug abuser but, in my own particular case, food was the focus of my destructive behaviour.

A victim or sufferer of anorexia becomes so wrapped up in their own little world that they can be perceived as wholly selfish. To a certain extent I agree with this thought as there is a huge element of selfishness if you think about all the heartache that is caused to the sufferer’s family and friends. Not only does this illness try to destroy the sufferer, but everyone else involved becomes affected and it takes an awful amount of strength and support to overcome these emotions. The contradictory aspect of this, however, is that anorexia is at the same time a very selfless illness. I know from my own experience the guilt I have felt through causing those around me so much upset; But throughout it all, I have felt far more compassion and pity for those I am hurting than towards myself.

The way I have learnt to see this illness is that I am not really worthy of receiving help, treatment and love and not worthy of the intake of food. Anorexia is all about control and once the control has been taken away everything becomes very frightening. The ironic thing is, however, that the anorexia itself becomes an enemy which is disguising itself as a friend and slowly but surely begins to control you. It is not something that you are consciously aware of, but nevertheless it grabs you with its powerful claws and once you are there it is very difficult to escape its clutch. It can also become an almost unbreakable habit and a way of life. If you live your life being ruled and controlled by this illness for long enough, it is quite easy to accept it as the norm and become too used to living this way. To break any habit, you need to discover another habit to replace it, though to find a new habit is not an easy task. Just as the smoker lights up a cigarette after each meal, the anorexic becomes used to not eating at certain times and avoiding particular foods. It is not always a conscious effort but becomes part of who you are and what you do.

Who can be brutally honest with themselves and put their hand on their heart and say that food does not affect some aspect of their life? If you feel depressed, it is very easy to begin eating for comfort or perhaps lose one's appetite. Food is an integral part of life and is used in dozens of different ways. Almost as soon as we emerge from the womb, we cry because we require feeding. When we are infants, we are cajoled into behaving ourselves by the bribery of sweets or something that tastes nice. We are told to eat our greens otherwise we will not have a pudding or biscuit for afters. I believe that most people use or abuse food in some form or another, but it is the extreme way that a person suffering with eating distress uses food that makes an everyday action become dangerously addictive.

I grew up in a stable background with loving parents and, up until my early twenties, had plenty of friends who I thought I could rely on. I was bullied at junior school, and I had an unhappy time at secondary school and a series of completely disastrous relationships when it came to boys and men. These factors are simply part and parcel of growing up and living in the real world, but unfortunately, I had a series of knock-backs which I misinterpreted and used food and the desire to be thinner than anyone else around me as a way of coping and blocking out memories and situations which I chose to forget. I desperately wanted to be liked and needed the opposite sex to find me attractive and I shall give just one example of how my longing for affection backfired on me and left me hating myself for a very long time.

He came from an exceedingly wealthy public-school background and lived in a different world. I was flattered that someone like him could possibly be interested in me as I was not used to a lifestyle of expensive cars and cocktail parties. In the eighties, his family and friends were what were known as classic 'Hooray Henry's' – all waxed coats and green wellies! He was the perfect snob and looked down on everyone. It intrigued me, and I found it all a complete novelty. I loved getting dressed up to go to dinner parties and loved chatting to men who thought they were lady killers when in fact they were utter prats!

I think it was with Jack (not his real name) that I experienced my first panic attack. Obviously, I didn't recognise it as such at the time, but looking back on how I felt and remembering the symptoms it seems highly likely that this is what I was going through. I think that I felt over-awed at this flash lifestyle that I was becoming part of and although part of me wanted to join in another part of me knew that it didn't suit my personality and just wasn't for me. The first major party that I attended with him was a summer ball held at his old school. We travelled a hundred miles or so to reach the venue and we were going to stay overnight in a hotel. I had bought my first ball gown which I fervently hoped would be what was expected of me to wear. I had been to Debenhams to buy it, although I lied to him and told him it had come from somewhere far more exclusive! I changed into my gorgeous new outfit, and he got changed into his dinner jacket and we went from the pre-ball drinks at his former house-master's house.

I was dreadfully nervous about this, which was made worse by the fact that Jack had told his friends that my father had a country house in Scotland and went deer hunting! That may sound quite amusing, but if you knew my father, it is more so, as he could never bear to touch my pet hamster without feeling squeamish, let alone shoot a live animal. We arrived at the house-master's residence, and I was introduced to lots of people, all very well spoken and immaculately dressed. I began to feel so nervous that I stopped being able to hear what people were saying to me and started getting so hot and dizzy that I knew I was going to pass out unless I got some fresh air. Jack took me to the door to take in some air and I was promptly sick in the garden's rockery. Instead of gaining any sympathy or compassion, Jack could not bear this humiliation and ordered a taxi to take us back to the hotel. I remember apologising over and over again saying that I had just been too hot, but in retrospect I believe that shear nerves and anxiety had caused me to react in this way. We arrived at the hotel, and Jack took me upstairs after which, to my immense horror and upset, he left to re-join the summer ball. He didn't return until about five o'clock the following morning and fell into bed without even asking me how I was feeling.

At that time, I was attending technical college on day release and for a couple of hours in the evening to learn typing and shorthand etc. as I had started working for my dad and wanted to prove that I had something to offer with qualifications. Parking was always difficult on an evening, and I generally had to park my car some distance from the college, although there was a subway which made the walk a lot shorter. One night, I was leaving night-school at about eight o'clock in the evening and headed for the subway. As I got about halfway through the underpass, three youths came around the corner towards me running from side to side. I was slightly apprehensive but kept my head down and decided that as I was nearer to the exit than the entrance, I would keep on walking towards the car park. These lads were acting in a stupid manner, and it began to look as though they were going to walk in my way or shout abuse at me, but one of them grabbed me and the other two started grappling with my bag and my coat. At this point, I reckoned that they were mugging me and did not try to stop them getting at my bag, in fact I would gladly have given it them. Then it became clear that they did not want my bag, but me and one of them was trying to grab the belt on my jeans. I was glad that it was wintertime and that I was not wearing anything more accessible, my thick coat and jeans proved somewhat of a problem for them. I heard more footsteps echoing along they subway although it was hard to determine which way they were coming from, and I had no idea whether they would belong to an accomplice or an ally. The only thing I remember next is kicking as hard as I could with my left leg and I definitely kick one of my assailants, though I don't where I kicked him. They ran off like frightened rabbits, probably at the thought of someone else approaching rather than my kick but at least they were gone. I didn't wait to see who else was walking along and instead I ran to my car and drove off.

I was due to meet Jack at his local pub, which was something I did every Monday evening after night school, and I couldn't wait to get to him. I was still shaking as I walked into the pub, but Jack was in a foul mood and hardly looked at me on my arrival. He started going on about the terrible day he had had at 'work' (a word with which he was unfamiliar in its rightful context), but nevertheless moaned about all sorts of things. I sat there at the bar with him listening to him for as long as I could and then just burst into tears much to the barmaid's surprise. He asked me what the matter was, and I started to tell him about the ordeal I had just endured. Before I had time to tell him the full story, he asked me if I had been raped. I said no and his response was "Thank god, we don't need to go to the police." That hadn't even crossed my mind at this point, I had just had the shock of my life and just felt as though I wanted a hug. He took me away from the bar into a corner of the pub and said; “If you ever tell anyone about tonight, I swear to god I’ll have your flaming legs broken!”

When I think about this now, it sounds preposterous that someone could have reacted this way, or that I should have taken him seriously, but the thought of what he could do with the type of company he kept frightened me enough never to tell even my best friend years after the event. I completely blocked it from my mind and nowadays it feels as though it happened to somebody else, even though I can remember that walk through the subway very clearly.

A couple of weeks or so later, Jack finished with me, and I was absolutely heartbroken. It didn’t last long, however as he came back to me begging to be forgiven, swamping me with bouquets of flowers, cuddly toys and other various presents including a very expensive gold bracelet. He had bought me jewellery in the past, but this was the most exclusive. Like an idiot, I fell for his charming ways, went back to him and the whole process began again leaving me feeling worthless, fat, and ugly. In the end, I finished the relationship when he announced that he was going on holiday with one of his friends. I decided that enough was enough, he demanded the bracelet back. I threw it at him and never encountered him again.

After Jack, I had a series of disastrous relationships but, finally, I met someone who was really a soulmate and we understood each other. He knew that I was insecure and had a ‘hang-up’ about my weight, but he was the most patient and tolerant person I have ever met. However, because I had been through such a lot previously, I was emotionally drained and unable to give him anything in return and so I finally ended up driving him away. I simply felt that I did not deserve such a kind considerate man. Because of the low self-esteem, lack of self-confidence and feelings of worthlessness, I somehow turned all these feelings inwards and set out on a self-destructive path ending up in hospital on two separate occasions and here I talk about the difference and similarities of the NHS and private health care systems.

After a few sessions of seeing a psychiatrist and a behavioural psychotherapist, I was admitted to our local psychiatric hospital as an in-patient. I had once seen a psychiatrist here before who had told me that I needed to pull my socks up and accept that I was growing up! This made me feel rather apprehensive, but I was assured that this particular person had long since left the hospital. Both my family and me were advised that this was the best course of action and we willingly agreed. Here, we were told, there would be qualified staff to help me gain weight and help me to find ways of thinking more positively. My behavioural psychotherapist (John) was wonderful with me and promise to visit me on the ward as often as he could.

There were tears as my parents said goodbye to me and I was shown to my room. I was grateful at the time that I had a room all to myself when most other patients seemed to be allocated beds onwards. I was weighed, given blood tests, asked the usual question for admittance purposes and went back to my room. I was told that for the first few days the staff would monitor my behaviour without intervening just to see how much I was actually eating. This was wonderful news to me. I could eat as little as I liked and not have anyone nagging at me or getting upset. My first meal arrived at tea-time and a nurse brought it into my room. On my plate were fish fingers, chips, and mushy peas. Obviously, I left every scrap of it. I hadn't eaten chips for months and everything on the plate as far as I was concerned spelt out FAT. A little later, a nurse came into the room and, surprised that I hadn't touched any food, asked if I was not hungry. I said I wasn't, and she took the plate and left. My room was right outside the nurses' station, and I later heard two of the nurses laughing at the fact that they had actually given an anorexic chips when my diet sheet had stated I ought to have had a salad.

I stayed in my room as long as I could, but eventually the craving for a cigarette got too much and I had to venture into the 'lounge' where patients were permitted to smoke. The first patient I encountered was an Iranian who spoke very little English. He was talking very quickly to me, and I hadn't a clue what he was trying to say. He was holding his hand out at was getting angrier and angrier. I was saved any more of this as a nurse came up to him and ushered him away telling me that I mustn't be bullied into giving him a cigarette or change for the telephone. I carried on and walked into the smoking lounge to face my fellow 'inmates'.

One lady walked through the room dragging her handbag behind her growling and making dog-like noises. Her handbag was evidently a dog for the time being and this put a completely different light on the phrase barking mad! I looked around the room and noticed that the door frames were damaged and there was a huge hole in one wooden panel. A friendly man next to me explained that the previous week a fight had broken out and one young man had gone berserk and tried to tear the place down with his bear-like hands. I was grateful that I had seated myself to a friendly person. We talked for a while, and he told me he had been suffering severe depression. He then introduced me to a couple of less intimidating people and told me if I had a problem to talk to them. He explained that I was bound to feel frightened on my first day, but that I would get used to it all. He was in fact very helpful and explained the trolley rota in which we were to take turns in taking food up to the dining room and the washing up rota that nobody took any notice of at all. The two of us spent a lot of our time in the kitchen washing up as no-one else wanted to do it and it was a way of escaping our environment for a while.

I don't mean to make fun of the people that were my fellow patients as they were some of the most disturbed and unstable people I am ever likely to encounter. I understand that they needed a lot of support but let me give you an idea of how it looked from my point of view.

One lady was a manic-depressive and would not speak at all for the first few days I was in the hospital. The next moment, she was talking ten to the dozen about her sex life in the most graphic details that made my stomach churn. She had a wicked sense of humour and from time to time made me laugh, but the sight of the scar across her throat from a previous suicide attempt put a somewhat of a damper on her humour.

Then there was a cross-dressed young man who had been caught trying to use the ladies' bathroom and had to be persuaded that this was causing the female patients distress. He protested, but agreed, and was eventually also persuaded to replace the skirt and blouse he was wearing with jumper and trousers. There was one occasion when a girl about my own age was brought in screaming and kicking and was eventually sedated. She later told us that her parents had called the doctors to her house because she had been drawing some sort of circles in her living room and carrying out some form of religious ceremonies which involved candles and glasses of whiskey! The mind boggled, but her parents had been concerned for the welfare of her little boy who lived with her.

One lad arrived late one night and introduced himself the next morning. He had driven himself to the hospital and told us that he was in a bit of bother with the police and some other lads near where he lived. He had had to return to the hospital to get away from them. His plan of action was that he would confess to hearing voices inside his head telling him to do bad things. When he felt as though things were quieting down on the outside, he would say that the voices were getting better and be discharged. He said this all quite as a matter of fact and admitted that he did this every once in a while. On evening, he went missing along with another woman, but they were soon picked up and returned by the police as she had her name shaved in the back of her head and they were both wearing NHS slippers.

One evening was particularly frightening as there was banging and crashing in the ward behind mine. A girl in her mid-twenties was going absolutely mad screaming and crying over the fact that she had been brought into hospital and was had only given birth a few days ago. I thought this was awful. How could someone be physically dragged like that away from her child? Then I learnt that she had four other children who had either been adopted or were in care. She later decided that she didn't want her newly born little girl after all and soon perked up. One boy sympathised with her admitting that he had a couple of kids somewhere and although he wasn't sure what sex they were, he thought one was a girl, or 'bitch' to use his own words.

I was far luckier than a lot of the patients as my parents came to see me virtually every evening. I looked forward to these visits like you wouldn't believe. Many people had no visitors at all and inevitably felt worried about being discharged back into society to return to their temporary bed and breakfast accommodation or hostel. My mum and dad frequently looked heart broken when visiting time was over. It was an awful ordeal for them, and I felt for them immensely. There was a special visiting room which was a huge sparse room dotted with a few big tatty plastic chairs. To say that the sounds of screaming and shouting and the banging that they heard were terrifying would be an understatement. I was also visited by some work colleagues and an ex-boyfriend, who was incredibly patient with me.

In the hospital, there was a pay phone, and I received a few calls from friends who wanted to visit me. I asked them not to. Not because I didn't want to see them, but the pure humiliation I felt at being in hospital was unbearable. I hated the thought of others seeing me like this. Certain friends understood my wishes and wrote letters, but there were some people who came to see me, which really distressed me no end especially when I realised that they had not really come to see me but had come to see what a psychiatric unit was really like. They constantly asked me what other people were in for and what they were like. These were the friends who took little or no notice of me when I was discharged, and one even crossed the road right in front of me, so he didn't have to make conversation with me.

Each day, I was visited by John, my therapist, and he kept to his word by visiting most working days. I lived for his visits, however short, as they broke up the monotony of my dreary days. Together we built up a very strong trusting relationship, and I was grateful for his concern and care for me. He didn't particularly talk to me about my problems, but helped me through the days by telling me about his wife and where they had been on nights out etc.

After four days, the doctors decided that I had been monitored enough and I was weighed again. To their surprise, I had lost rather a lot of weight. The fact that I had been left to eat entirely what I wanted (which was hardly anything) did not seem to cross their minds and armed with the details of my weight I was summoned to see the consultant psychiatrist. I was told that unless I gained weight, I would be but on 'bed-rest' which meant that I would have to spend my days in bed and be closely watched at mealtimes. They told me I was to eat three meals a day and also drink three Build-Up drinks, which are basically meal supplements containing necessary vitamins etc. I agreed to this and went out of the door.

Shortly afterwards, I was called in again to see a doctor I had not seen before. I sat down and one of the male nurses accompanied me. I was then subjected to a series of questions which I found most peculiar. They were all sex orientated, for example how did I feel about the male patients on the ward, did I feel sexually attracted to them? His questions became more and more personal, and I felt so embarrassed I wanted the ground to swallow me up, but I thought that perhaps I was being tested on my ability to cope with embarrassment or something, so I simply answered what I was asked. In any other situation, I would have told my interrogator where to go, but I felt most intimidated and did not even dare look up at the male nurse as I found everything so horribly awkward. After the questions, I was allowed to go. I began walking back up the corridor and another nurse called me back saying that the doctor needed to check my lithium levels. I told her I wasn't even taking lithium. She checked her notes and quickly realised that the doctor had been speaking to the wrong patient! I was rapidly beginning to lose the little faith I had in everyone there!

After about three weeks, I still hadn't gained any more weight and was told that I wouldn't be able to go home for a week-end visit if I did not put some on. I decided there and then that I had been there too long and made up my mind to discharge myself. I was getting no help whatsoever, and no one was offering me any real therapy. The nurses were wonderfully friendly and kind, but not equipped to deal with someone with anorexia. They could deal with sedating a schizophrenic, but actually helping someone recover from a problem like mine was not on the agenda. For a start, there were not enough members of staff to concentrate on the intense counselling that I required, and the time spent on me would have taken up too many hours that were needed restraining other patients.

It was all very frightening and the people I was in daily contact with were very intimidating. Patients smoked cannabis in the entrance of the hospital and because the main automatic doors were frequently opening, the smell would quickly float outside, although it did not take a genius to realise that the smell on people's clothes after they had smoked was not just plain nicotine. Many of the patients suffering with alcoholism had been admitted to hospital for a 'drying out' period, yet they would tell a nurse they were going for a walk and head straight for the nearest pub. I witnessed this myself, smelt the drink on their breath and saw the cans of lager or bottles of cider they brought back with them. Security measures were certainly not a strong point of the hospital at that time.

There was one very large lady who grabbed me round the neck and started telling me I was evil, and she began to quote the Bible to me. She told me to look up a particular chapter and verse and then I would be saved. Everyone had a copy of the Bible next to their beds and so I looked it up feeling as though if I did so, things would be alright. The chapter and verse did not even exist. On another occasion, one girl who was about ten times my size demanded I gave her some of my cigarettes. I obliged and she seemed truly grateful, but after about the sixth time of her asking I was brave enough to refuse. Happily, all I got was a mouthful of verbal abuse and I thanked my lucky starts that she hadn't decided to become physically violent as she had previously done with some of the nursing staff. My bed was next to hers and on an evening, I used to lie on my bed and listed to the radio on my Sony

Walkman. She used to complain that I was being too noisy and used to come round and turn out my light so that I couldn't read my magazines. I didn't object or retaliate which was probably the wisest move.

Eventually I told one of the nurses that I really had enough. I was in a bad state. I wasn't sleeping properly and was thoroughly depressed and not getting any better. The nurse told me that as I had come into hospital voluntarily, I was completely entitled to discharged myself, but she added that as I was signing myself out, the doctors would be signing papers to section me under the Mental Health Act so I might as well get on with it and make the best of it until I was officially allowed to go home. I should never have been threatened or emotionally blackmailed in this manner, but I was scared, naïve and desperate to get home as quickly as possible.

As time went on, the relationship I had built up with John, my therapist, seemed to deteriorate. He appeared to be less communicative with me and stopped cracking jokes to cheer me up. One morning, I was called in to see the psychiatrist and was informed that I was not going to get better in hospital and that I was to go home. This news came like a bolt out of the blue. I was flabbergasted to say the least as I had received no hint or prior warning that I was going to be discharged. I was told that I was giving out confusing and mixed messages to the staff and they could not help me whilst I remained in hospital. I really didn't understand at all, but certainly declined from questioning or arguing the accusations as I was desperate to return home. I was told however that I must attend the hospital as an outpatient several times a week to attend group therapy sessions and occupational therapy. I joyfully agreed and ran down to the telephone to break the news to my mum.

I think the whole family was delighted that I had finally been 'released' after seven weeks of what I can only describe as sheer hell, but in the same breath it was seven weeks of wasted valuable time that had served none of the intended purpose. I was a lot thinner, a lot more depressed and my self-confidence, which had been at an all-time low seven weeks before, was even lower. I felt ashamed, embarrassed and imagined that people could almost see a straightjacket on me and 'I've just been to a lunatic asylum' stamped across my forehead. Going back home was a strange experience, I almost felt like a guest in my own home. Mum and dad were treating me as though I was likely to crack at any time and the atmosphere was tense. They didn't want to push me too hard at mealtimes but didn't want to leave me to my own devices and let me eat exactly what I wanted (or didn't want).

Obediently, I attended the daytime sessions up at the hospital and I may as well have attended a daytime crèche. I was supposed to be receiving therapy, but I felt as though I was living my life again at playschool. Once, I turned up to a group to discover that we had a choice of whether to make bird-boxes or key ring holders out of bits of wood that simply required gluing together. On another occasion, we made pictures out of scraps of material and amusing faces using crayons and paper plates. This may have stimulated the mind of a three-year-old child, but it hardly seemed as though it was going to help me understand my illness and its accompanying problems. We also had to write short stories based on a particular theme, then read them to the rest of the group. An example of this was the time we had to write about who we would most like to be trapped in a lift with. This was terribly exciting to the gentlemen with sexual hang-ups who went into great detail about Nicole Kidman and Raquel Welch.

The discussions groups were no more productive from my own point of view. We were told that we could discuss anything we wished... except for our illnesses, religion or politics. The latter two I can manage without, but I would have thought that actually talking about our illnesses or problems could have been interesting, helpful, and therapeutic. After several weeks of tolerating these groups and sessions, I decided that I had not benefited and was thoroughly fed up. John the therapist had ceased to visit me, and I had no appointments with him at all. I took it upon myself to throw in the towel and admit defeat. I told one of the girls who ran the daytime sessions that I would not be returning and was promptly told that I could not pack it in just like that. I would have to see a doctor to see whether it was appropriate. I repeated that I was not returning and turned my back on her and the hospital for good as far as I was concerned.

I was recently required quite to see a psychiatrist who worked on the same ward where I had been a patient. As I walked towards the ward, I lost my bearings and had to ask for directions. I thought for a moment that I had arrived in the wrong place because things seemed so different. Chairs and televisions were in different places, there were paintings on the once bare walls and carpets lined in the once long cold corridors. The rooms had been redecorated and painted in more subtle pastel colours. I presume this was to encourage a somewhat more calming sedating atmosphere. The staff no longer wore crisp uniforms but walked around in their own clothes. After a while, however, I realised that I was not mistaken and that it was the same ward having undergone a facelift. As I waited in the corridor for the psychiatrist to meet me, I witnessed some patients walking past me and the memories of my weeks as an in-patient came flooding back. It was quite surreal. One man emerged from his room walking in a most peculiar manner and then in front of everyone began laughing whilst putting his hands down his trousers and masturbating. Another woman walked around asking the staff if they could explain what was happening to her because she felt confused and muddled. I realised with horror that this poor woman had been a patient with me eleven years ago. This confirmed my thoughts on the place, and I was still as scared now as I had been before. I realised that all the wallpaper, paint and carpets in the world could not cover up or conceal something which will never alter. The patients may come and go, but nothing about NHS psychiatric care really changes.

I tried on my own to get my life back into to some semblance of order but found things very hard. I had no support (bad or good) and did not gain any weight or face any of the things that had caused my problems. My then GP (who has now since left the practice) was shocked to see me still looking as poorly if not worse than when I had been admitted into hospital months before. This was the same GP who had, a long time ago, assured my mum that I did not have an eating disorder and that it was just my age! After phone calls here and everywhere, she eventually came up with the name of a psychiatrist from

Altrincham. Luckily for me, I was in a private health care scheme and was able to see her almost straight away. I arrived for this appointment on a cold October morning feeling very sceptical and in a somewhat defensive non-committal frame of mind.

The psychiatrist was very pleasant and made me feel like a person who had a problem that could be addressed. I had not felt like this before and she assured me that she could help me in some way. She informed me that I needed to attend the hospital as an inpatient and one of the members of staff showed both me and my mother round some of the building. One has to bear in mind of course that when I had been in hospital before all I saw were sparse wards and long corridors. This was a private establishment and no expense seemed to be spared. Nowadays, the Priory Hospital group is more commonly related to pop stars, actors, and other famous celebrities, but at the time I had never heard of the place. I was asked not to make any decisions that day but was sent home with the hospital telephone number and a very plush brochure describing the picturesque scenery and the luxurious surroundings. The grounds of the hospital in Cheshire were beautiful as were all the houses nearby. Many were virtually mansions. Lots of famous people lived close by and the road leading towards the Priory reeked of affluence. There was nothing to consider, really. I had made my mind up there and then and on our return home, my mum made the phone call to say that I had decided that I would attend as an inpatient.

Taking a look around my room, I soon saw that it was a far cry from the ward I had been on my previous stay in hospital. Here, I had my own wardrobe, dressing table, cupboards, bedside table and a very comfortable looking bed with matching quilt and pillow slips. There was a television and even a telephone. I went to investigate the bathroom only to discover it was locked. I ventured outside my room to find a nurse who unlocked it for me. I got changed and, several minutes later, the nurse returned and re-locked the bathroom door. She told me that my bathroom door would remain locked until I had spoken with the psychiatrist. I was rather taken aback and stunned at this strange decision but did not question it and unpacked the rest of my clothes. I was soon summoned to see the psychiatrist who explained how my treatment would begin and how my days were going to be structured. I had no idea what lay ahead.

She started on the subject of food. First thing, each morning I was to be weighed and my weight would be marked on a chart but not disclosed to me. I was to stand with my back to the scales and would not be told how much I weighed until I was ready to accept that I was putting on weight. I was to gain weight weekly and if there was no weight gain then they would investigate as to the reason why and discover how I was cheating or manipulating their system of working. I would be expected to eat breakfast, lunch and dinner with three snacks in between and drink a pint of milk each day. The thought of this as she was telling me was absolutely horrendous. I could not imagine anything worse than someone telling me what and when to eat and the amounts I would be eating sounded terrifying. I managed to stop myself from crying and concentrated on what she was telling me. For the first couple of days, I would be served quarter portions, then half portions and finally progress to full portions. This was so that my body could adjust to eating normally again. When you have not eaten much or regularly for a long time, the stomach shrinks, so increasing the amount of food intake gradually was the best way to overcome this problem and cause me minimum discomfort.

To begin with, I was to eat in a separate dining from the rest of the patients. It was a room that was specifically for the patients on the eating disorder programme, but at that moment in time I was the only patient on this programme. I was to sit in this room for an hour after each main meal and for thirty minutes after each snack to let my body digest the food and to contemplate my feelings. I would be issued with a diary in which I was to record how I felt about myself, my body image and anything else I wished to talk about. Apart from writing in the diary, I was not permitted to read anything, or do any other activity until my time was up. I would not be allowed to take any form of exercise at all and would not even be permitted to go on walks for at least a couple of weeks. I was told that the nurses would be looking out for me in case I tried to exercise in my room.

When I wanted to use the toilet, I was to inform a nurse who would unlock my door and stand outside watching me to ensure that I wasn't making myself sick or somehow disposing of food in any other way. This was just too much, and I argued that there would be no way I could possibly use the toilet with someone watching but was told I would get used to it. I could not bear the thought of all this food and being made to eat at set times. I told this to Dr Salmon who tried to console me by telling me I was allowed to have three "dislikes", meaning I could name three foods that I did not wish to eat. It must have amused her greatly telling each patient this as most patients would undoubtedly insist that they were either vegetarians or vegans and include foods such as chips, cream, butter, milk and cheese in their disliked foods. Unfortunately for us, however, these were not permitted, although I was allowed to be vegetarian (except for fish). I said I could not decide on my dislikes and would think about it.

My days during the week were to consist of rather intense therapy including talking about what I had written in my diary, talking with a therapist, learning to become more assertive and confident, overcoming my distorted body image and learning relaxation techniques. I was not permitted any visits for the first week, but from thereon after, I was allowed two weekly visits on a weekend and was allowed to make or take three phone calls a week and the number of calls I made would be monitored by the switchboard operator. After I had started eating normally again, I would be allowed the 'privilege' of making up my own snacks and would eventually be allowed into the main dining room to dine with the other residents. My psychiatrist then sent me back to my room to absorb what I had been told. I lay down on my bed and sobbed. There seemed to be no escape from this awfully strict daily regime. I thought carefully and decided that I would try really hard to get better by doing what was required of me and made up my mind that I would put on the weight they wanted, get discharged and go immediately on a diet once I returned home. In the back of my mind, I had decided that if things got too bad to cope with, I could always kill myself. I had actually come prepared for that by hiding some old anti-depressants in the bottom of my suitcase, it was just a precautionary measure, but one I was prepared to take should things become unbearable.

Presently, a nurse came to inform me that it was lunch time. I could go on and on about the amounts of food I was served up with, but I won't. All I can say was that I was amazed that this first meal was supposed to be a 'quarter' portion! There was a salad, coleslaw, tuna, and a bread roll with an individual portion of butter on the plate. I had to place all the butter on the roll, scraping every last blob of it onto the bread and was informed that there would be two rolls on the full portions. For afters there was a piece of fruit. I sat for an hour afterwards feeling absolutely bloated, fat, uncomfortable and miserable although I held back any tears deciding to save them for later when I was by myself. Mid-afternoon was snack time, and this would generally consist of either a biscuit or jam and bread. The main meal of the day was served in the evening and was the meal which the other girls that were to later join me and I hated the most. Invariably there were loads of potatoes; mashed, boiled, chipped, rice, pasta, cheese and everything seemed to be swimming in grease and fat. They were all the foods that someone suffering from anorexia would avoid like the plague. Instead of seeing the food for what it was, we would just see the fat content and start totting up the calories. There was usually something equally as fattening and disgusting for pudding; Either sponge puddings, cakes with cream in and ice cream. Just before bedtime came the last snack of the day, usually a biscuit or hot chocolate and the opportunity to finish off the pint of milk we hadn't managed to stomach during the day. The breakfasts would comprise a bowl of cereal followed by two slices of toast. On each slice of toast, I had to fit on a portion of butter and a portion of jam/marmalade. This may not seem so dreadful for the average person but fitting it all on was an art in itself, and then the actual act of eating it was sickening. The mid-morning snack would consist of a piece of fruit or a chocolate biscuit and so the cycle started again. It seemed to be a never-ending flow of mealtimes and drinks.

From a psychological point of view, this was a horrible experience as the feeling of self-hate and loathing seemed to increase on a daily basis. From a physical point of view, it felt even worse. Even when I was underweighting from not eating enough, I felt fat, but now with all this food inside me I felt even worse and at times could barely stand upright from feeling so full. Unfortunately, when you begin to put weight on at a rather quick rate, the weight does not have time to distribute itself evenly and therefore seems to stick on the stomach and thighs. I used to stand in front of the mirror on an evening I truly looked as if I was eight months pregnant. Going to the toilet was posing an awful problem as well. It is most disconcerting to perform bodily functions whilst someone stands outside the bathroom door keeping their eye on you. I usually had to run the tap and close my eyes to pretend there was nobody around.

Being isolated from the rest of the residents was a lonely experience and I felt like some sort of leper when I was allowed to stand at the reception door to watch the bonfire night celebrations whilst everyone else had invited friends and relatives. A couple of weeks later, I was joined by four other girls. We were all in the same boat although did not necessarily suffer from exactly the same disorder. In them, I found a close friendship, the camaraderie was amazing we could completely and utterly empathise with each other for this I will always be grateful. We all hated the way we looked, and we all shared the same disgust and repulsion for the food we had to eat regardless of whether we actually liked it. Of course, the fact was that it was all out of our control, and we had no say in the matter. However, 'Where there is a will, there is a way', so they say, and I always agreed with the assumption that rules were meant to be broken. Each night, the five of us would congregate in my bedroom and talk about all sorts of things and, once we were allowed to know it, we would compare our weight gain.

One girl (I shall call her Ruth) had discovered that upstairs there was a toilet that was unlocked (presumably it was for visitors) and that she had visited this toilet on several occasions and made herself sick. From then on, me and her used to visit this tiny room and for a while managed to mystify the staff with our lack of weight gain. It was a huge victory to be weighed each morning only to be told that there was no change. The sense of 'winning' was overwhelming. Eventually, however, in a discussion group, Ruth admitted our misdemeanour, the upstairs toilet door was locked and for a while we both felt relieved that we no longer had to lie. The relief did not last long, and we both regretted her ever having opened her mouth. As time went on, we were allowed to make our own snacks which was seen as a huge breakthrough, and it meant that the staff were finally beginning to trust us. We obviously broke the trust as we had access to the locked kitchen and used this opportunity to water down our daily pints of milk and pretend we had eaten a Kit-Kat or had some jam on our bread. As we continued to trick the nursing staff, we were all gradually allowed into the main lounge and conversed with other patients. These people mainly suffered from drink and drug addiction. They were all really nice people and we all seemed to get on with each other very well. We all knew that each of us had problems, and I must say that most of the alcoholics I met were well on the road to recovery by the time they left the hospital.

Eventually we members of the eating disorder gang were allowed to venture up to the dining room for our lunch. It was decked out like an exclusive hotel and the food was (for those that enjoy eating) a wonderful buffet. We were always accompanied by a nurse, but it was relatively easy to distract her and so whilst one of us would be talking to her, or showing her something or other, one of us would be hurriedly shovelling food into serviettes on our laps or hiding it under the table covers! This clearly was not the way in which any of us were going to get better, but the main aim in our eyes was to defeat the system and regain our control over the situation. With hindsight I would go back tomorrow if I could and recover far more easily, but the reality of what not getting better meant than was very different from what it means to me now. The long-term implications of anorexia and other eating disorders did not matter to any of us. We just lived for the present moment in time and were uninterested in what may happen in the future. Had I known that I would have suffered as much as I have done, I would have made a concerted effort to stick to the rigorous regime and try my hardest to learn from the experience.

Gradually, we were allowed to go for short walks around the hospital grounds and neighbouring country lanes. Naturally, we were accompanied by a nurse in ensure that we did not start doing cartwheels or break into a sprint in order to burn off those ugly calories. These walks were wonderful and the freedom of being allowed outside in the fresh air very welcoming. As part of our therapy, we were to go on a shopping expedition, which meant that for the first time in weeks we were to go into civilisation, talk to 'real' people and act as though we were regular members of society again. We were to go shopping for clothes and buy at least one item to wear. For me, this meant that for the first time in a long while I tried on clothes in shops that sold adult sizes rather that wearing items from the children's departments. I tried on a pair of jeans and to my absolute horror and indignation, no matter how hard I squeezed into one particular pair, they just would not go round my hips. This realised my worst nightmare! I was a huge, bloated pig with thunder thighs and a great bulging backside. Reluctantly, I purchased the next size up and also bought a shirt to match. We then ventured off to the cafeteria where we had to have a drink and a cake. Nothing could have been worse at the time. Back at the hospital, my mood went into a serious decline as I felt so uncomfortable, ugly, worthless and totally miserable.

My next relief came when one of the cleaners who came into the rooms every morning accidentally left the bathroom door unlocked. My conscience told me to tell one of the staff, but my fat stomach told me that this was my way to lose some of this fat slowly creeping all over my body. I told no one for a few days and each morning as I was weighed it was discovered that my weight was going down slightly. I denied any knowledge as to why and for a while nobody could understand it.

Unfortunately, I left the door slightly off the catch one evening and a nurse coming in to administer my medication noticed it and that was that. By this time, I had been in the hospital for almost two months and Christmas was approaching. For a special treat, we were to be allowed to go home to visit on Christmas Day, although I asked if I could go on Boxing Day instead as it was my birthday. Returning home after such a long time was a strange experience and it was very difficult for the whole family. They wanted everything to be as normal as possible but didn't want to say or do anything that would upset me so they must have felt as though they were treading on eggshells.

The period between Christmas and New Year was devastatingly depressing. A couple of the other girls had been discharged and I missed them terribly as we had become very close. I decided that there was only one thing to do and that was to die. I had been craftily saving up my sleeping tablets for the past fortnight by pretending to swallow them, then placing them in a pocket of my teddy bear. One day just prior to the evening meal, I decided that I had taken as much as I could bear and one by one, I swallowed the sleeping pills along with a few anti-depressants thrown in for good measure. I reckoned that by the time they started to work, I would be able to say that I was tired, go to bed early and never wake up. Luckily or unluckily (depending on which way you look at it), the tablets took effect extremely quickly and in the middle of eating my meal I was aware of people asking me if I was alright. I remember swaying and trying to stand up only to be supported by a nurse. The next thing I knew was that those around me were telling me to try and keep my eyes open and stay awake. I didn't really know what was happening, all I felt was as though I was really, really drunk.

Shortly afterwards, I was in an ambulance being carted off to the nearest A&E department. I have very little recollection about the events that followed, although I remember a pipe being rammed down my throat and liquid being poured down it and me throwing up everywhere. I woke up the next morning attached to a drip and heart monitor feeling with a rather sore throat after having had my stomach pumped. A nurse came in with a drink for me which was charcoal based, presumably to absorb any remaining drugs in my body. The drink was vile, and my mouth was black for days afterwards. I was not in the hospital for long once it was discovered that I was a psychiatric in patient. I was checked over then a nurse came to collect me and take me back to the hell from which I had been trying to escape.

Returning to hospital was not easy as my new friends were extremely concerned at what I had done and the nurses although very understanding were very stern with me. My room had to be searched and nothing was left unturned. All my clothes were thoroughly checked, my bed was stripped right down and they even checked behind the pictures. I felt humiliated and ashamed of my actions. I had not thought or considered the other implications such as what all this would have done to my parents. I asked for them not to be told, but it was too late, they had been informed as soon as I had been taken into hospital and, on the doctor's advice, were going to come to visit me in a couple of days. I felt dreadful at what I had done but was sure that I would gain lots of sympathy from them and looked forward to their visit. It was by now New Years' Eve, and it was one of the most depressing I had ever had. I still felt weak and dizzy from my overdose and wanted to be with my family. Instead, I was wishing people I barely knew a 'happy new year'.

When my parents came to see me, I knew instantly by the look on their faces that I was not going to receive the sympathy I thought I merited. My mum was just thoroughly upset and bewildered, and my dad could hardly bear to look at me, let alone speak to me. Eventually he could not stand being in the same room and left us to go for a walk. I was told that what I had done was a stupid way to deal with things and they were obviously disappointed, frightened and concerned. All I could do was apologise and try to explain that I saw no other way out at the time. From then on, I was back to having all meals supervised and felt as though I was back at square one. I decided to try very hard indeed to make the effort to become well enough to be discharged and make things up with my parents.

I was thankfully discharged after just over twelve long weeks. The psychiatrist drew up what she termed a contract whereby I was to attend the hospital twice a week for therapy and to be weighed. I was not to lose any weight whatsoever and had to still keep writing in my diary about the way I felt about myself. In return for me keeping to my side of the contract she would continue to support and help me as much as she could. Thinking back, this was a very fair deal, but alas all I could think about was getting home and getting on a crash diet to alleviate myself from this awful body that was daily growing round me. On my return home, I began losing weight again and for the first time in many weeks felt back in control. I felt as though I was strong again and had the power to lose any weight I wanted. The reality of the situation was that the anorexia was completely and totally controlling me and the way I felt. As far as I was concerned, food was still such a huge issue with me and calorie counting gave me a buzz. I realise now that by doing this I was blocking real life out by focusing on my weight.

Inevitably I broke the contract, my psychiatrist agreed to keep seeing me on a weekly basis and she was in fact very helpful. She was a very astute woman and had a great deal of knowledge of eating disorders. She knew all the tricks in the trade, knew the pitfalls and sometimes I felt as though she was reading my mind. The majority of anorexics, when they are first treated, will say that they want to get better but they don't want to get fat. All they are saying is that they want to feel happy but need to maintain control on at least one aspect of their life.

There is no way someone of a very low weight can hope to 'get better' without weight gain. The less you eat, the more depressed you get, your mind starts to wander, short-term and long-term memory is poor, but as far as the anorexic is concerned getting well entails getting fat and this is just the last thing they want. Many will say that they do not argue with their parents apart from the issue of food. Naturally! They are masking every other possible problem by making food the issue so that nothing else can be talked about, thought about, or focused on. This is not true for everyone of course but it certainly is so for the other sufferers I have met and, I know so, for myself. The problem is to determine what problems are underlying and to find them is not always as simple as it may sound.

The hospital was at least an hour's drive away from my home, but I got used to the journey and at first did not have any problem with it. Then, for no logical explanation, I began to feel unwell every time I set out in the car. My head would start spinning, my eyesight would become blurred, and I broke out into uncontrollable sweats. On several occasions, I had to pull into the side of the road, but the worst times were those in traffic jams or when stationary at traffic lights, when there was nowhere to stop and sit for a while. These feelings I have now learnt are some of the symptoms experienced in an anxiety attack, but they are the most frightening sensations. At the time I just felt that I would either collapse unconscious at the wheel of my car or simply die there and then. The journeys to hospital became harder and harder, but I persevered with them knowing that at least when I arrived at my destination that I would feel better until it was time to leave and get back into the busy traffic.

One day at home, I opened my mail and to my shock and horror discovered that the private health care scheme was no longer prepared to cover the cost of my treatment for anorexia. They said that they would cover any other illnesses or hospital stays, but for this specific complaint they were going to give me another few weeks and then cease to insure me. I was mortified, although without the scheme in the first place I would not have been able to afford to stay in hospital for a week never mind twelve weeks plus all the aftercare. The cost would have run into many thousands of pounds, so I suppose it was not altogether unreasonable that the company should wish to end paying for all my treatment.

I do not believe that any person who has been the victim of an addictive mental illness is ever totally recovered. They may go into a form of remission, but their problems will always be present at the backs of their minds and certain situations, or events will be trigger points for their particular problem to rear its ugly head again. My anorexia will always be my 'Achilles' heel' and no matter how much I may recover in the future, I believe there will always be a part of me that will be susceptible to falling back into the evil trap.

At this particular time in my life and in my illness, I have finally found the support I have spent years hunting for. My rock has been my present GP who has provided me with medical support for about the past eighteen months. Without him, I would have sunk lower and lower, and I cannot say what I would have done. He has helped me through some of the most difficult times in my life and has always been there to listen and understand my predicament. On many occasions, I have been very distressed and have always been reassured that I was not losing my mind, though it felt as though I was, and he has always maintained contact with me on a regular basis. For this I am eternally grateful as in the years previously I have felt as though I have been passed from pillar to post with no regular contact or communication taking place and I always seemed to slip through the net, never receiving backup or support. In addition to treatment by my GP, I am still in touch with a consultant psychiatrist who always assures me that I will get better and that there is a light at the end of the tunnel.

I have also had the privilege to be counselled by the practice-based counsellor with whom I have built up an excellent honest, open and trusting relationship, and I attend a counselling group at the surgery run by another wonderful lady counsellor. My family, though this should go without saying, has been a constant power of support and their unconditional love has been enormous. I still find it difficult to come to terms with the fact that they feel I am worthy of so much care, love and devotion.

I often feel very bitter about the fact that I did not receive the correct treatment from the NHS when I was younger, and I know that I am not alone in feeling this way. Hopefully, the medical profession is learning to recognise symptoms of mental illnesses more quickly and there are far more drugs on the market than there ever used to be. Counselling does not carry the stigma it once did, and people are not quite as embarrassed at admitting that they have a psychological problem. Another distressing and upsetting factor of this horrible situation is that my problems have not just stopped at having anorexia and depression. There have been the most awful times in my life when I have felt as though I am suffering from cancer and dying and have virtually not been able to get out of bed. I have suffered with terrible stomach pains from either not eating the correct food or from making myself sick. I have endured countless hours of dental treatment as a poor diet and forced vomiting does nothing for healthy teeth. Some of them have begun to decay that therefore I have had to have them crowned, on other occasions I have suffered many abscesses which have been excruciatingly painful and only ever occur if I am particularly depressed and down. I have been warned about the dangers of osteoporosis which has not affected me yet but could well do in later life. I have also worried about the prospect of having children. For so many years, my periods have been either completely absent, or very erratic and painful and the thought of not being able to bear a child is very distressing.

I have moments of intense 'broodiness' whereby I look at babies, think about them and dream about them. What if I have damaged myself so much that I can never have one of my own? I can easily become worried about the fact that I will never find Mr Right. Who would want me with my past? Who would want me especially after reading this rather open account of my experiences? Who could bear to put up with someone like me? Maybe there is someone out there, I believe he exists, but he must be very special indeed, and I will never be truly happy until I have found him.

Will I ever recover? Does anyone really and truly recover from such things, or do they basically go into remission and know that it is something which will always be a part of them? In my opinion, I think the latter will apply. In any case, I have accomplished the task which I set out to do and have written this as part of my own therapy. Dismiss it as trash if you will or learn from it and maybe others will take heed and realise that there are other, better, and more constructive ways of dealing with the poor hand that life can deal. I am most certainly not on a pioneering crusade to shout about how to deal with eating disorders, depression and anxiety, but maybe one day someone will read just a part of this that will strike a chord and stop the preventable happening.

Prayer of Forgiveness

I forgive the tears I was made to shed,
I forgive the pain and the disappointments,
I forgive the betrayals and the lies,
I forgive the slanders and intrigues,
I forgive the hatred and the persecution,
I forgive the blows that hurt me,
I forgive the wrecked dreams,
I forgive the still-born hopes,
I forgive the hostility and jealousy,
I forgive the indifference and ill will,
I forgive the injustice carried out in the name of justice,
I forgive the anger and the cruelty,
I forgive the neglect and the contempt,
I forgive the world and all its evils?
I also forgive myself.
May the misfortunes of the past no longer weigh on my heart.
Instead of pain and resentment, I choose understanding and compassion.
Instead of rebellion, I choose artistic creation.
Instead of grief, I choose forgetting.
Instead of vengeance I choose victory.
I will be capable of loving regardless of whether I am loved in return,
Of giving even when I have nothing,
Of working happily even in the midst of difficulties,
Of holding out my hand even when utterly alone and abandoned,
Of drying my tears even while I weep,
Of believing even when no one believes in me.

Paulo Coelho, Aleph.

Buried Alive in the Blues

In February 2000, I took time off work for the first time ever. As a reasonably successful teacher of eight years, I had started taking anti-depressant tablets. However, in my opinion at least, I still thought that there was nothing really wrong with me. I was a person who, to the outside world, appeared to be able to cope with all the ups and downs and the stresses and strains of life both at home and in the classroom and staffroom at school. I had been promoted at the young age of twenty-six and managed to hold down a part time masters' degree course for three years whilst working full time. How could I be suffering from depression? The doctor had obviously got it wrong. Everything had just caught up with me; Moving house, moving schools, getting promoted. My life was one big upheaval. Who wouldn't have problems adjusting?

Yet for all of that month I found myself sitting helplessly in my front room, watching the rain pouring down on the hills through my window. I was in shock that I, with all my knowledge and ability, had been driven to see the doctor by my exasperated partner and that, on seeing me, the doctor had immediately signed me off work. He signed ME off! What was that about? Was I really ill? I mean, I didn't have a cold, or a broken bone and I wasn't confined to bed. With that all the greatest feelings of failure I had ever experienced in my professional life suddenly coming home to roost. What worried me more was where it left my home life. Was I really such a sad and miserable person to be around? I suffered a crisis of self-confidence. I couldn't face leaving the house in the mornings, not even making it out of bed on some occasions. Did I really dread my working day that much?

The following month, I found myself still off work. I wondered what to say to my boss each time he rang. The conversation would go like this; "Yes, they still think I'm depressed and yes, I'm still zonked out by these tablets. Yes, the doctor has upped the dose to try and see if it will speed things up and no, I have no idea when I will be back." I know they told me not to worry about my classes and the staff were coping, but I spent a lot of time feeling really guilty. After all, how could supply teachers really know what my class needed to get them motivated? I couldn't understand why a senior manager kept ringing me up because each time she did I felt I just couldn't talk to her. She just didn't get why I was off work in the first place. I just wanted to bury my head in the sand and forget I had any contact with my school. I simply didn't want to have to think about anything.

My family tried to be supportive in their own way but not in a way that seemed to help me to 'snap out of it'. Mum worried about me and kept popping in for the day to take me to the shops for 'lunch and a chat'. I felt that I was troubling her at a time when I knew that she wasn't well and was awaiting admission for surgery. My brother wrote to me. It was good to know that he was thinking about me. Nan told me that my Granddad once had a similar problem which only started me worrying that I might have some untreatable hereditary condition which was unavoidable and pre-destined. Dad promised to take me out for a long walk, which I really needed, but even walking, which I always enjoyed, did little to alleviate how I felt. I decided that, for my partner, I was not too nice a person to live with; Refusing to get out of bed, crying all the time or suffering dark moods. It was as if I were in a permanent PMT state. No-one's idea of domestic bliss!

Just before Easter, my best friend from college arrived to stay. I soon discovered that she was in a remarkably similar state to me. Parallel lives or what? We decided it was a late 20's/early 30's' career crisis disease. We went for a walk and put the world to rights – at least temporarily! Then we moved onto considering whether or not God existed – which was pathetic as I could not see how religion could help me to get out of my predicament. It had never done much for me before. I decided I would stick to my chemical cocktail and continued to take half the day to come to for the next few weeks. Two weeks before Easter, I decided to force myself to go back to work. I spent most of my time dreading it but told myself it was only two weeks until the holiday. Somehow, I got to Easter, but I hated my life even more, wondering why I'd ever decided to go back. The people were the same, my boredom levels exactly the same, but at least the kids were happy to see me back. My tablet regime remained stoutly difficult to control. I just couldn't wake up in the morning. Instead of giving me a lift they really knocked me out. As a result, I started to accept that maybe something was wrong or at least not quite right. From my previous 'nerves of steel' in the classroom, I had returned to work feeling very anxious, shaky and shattered.

I should not have been drinking with the tablets but some nights it seemed to help me calm down. Driving home from Leeds one night, however, I realised, just in time, that I had driven part way along one road completely on the wrong side, I could have put us both in hospital! We decided, after that, that I had better not drive home when I was tired, and I decided that I better not have any more alcohol.

Schooldays were, quite frankly, weird. Marking was a joke. Just making it there was an achievement in itself! Getting up and performing in front of a class was a further miracle. At break time, I distanced myself from other people as much as I could because I couldn't face being asked if I was alright now. By May, years eleven and thirteen had gone, which meant a bit less pressure, but I was just hanging on by a thread for the six weeks summer holiday. Then I had a two weeks break across the ocean and four weeks to chill. My masters' degree graduation was spent with my family but served to remind me of the old ambitious me. Where had my drive gone and why? I still needed it, but I just could not find it again.

Then a job opportunity came up at a local University. It was only part time – just two days a week but I didn't care. I became desperate to get it and got very worked up about asking my head for time off to go for the interview but, of course, he let me go. On the day, I realised I had reached the last three, and was in with a good chance but I felt I'd received all too familiar feedback when I didn't get it in the end; 'I was the wrong side of 30, and despite having talent, I lacked enough years of experience'. It was just like the way that many other positions in the teaching profession are awarded. The whole experience spun me out of control, and I felt as if I was thrown, spiralling backwards as I faced having to stay put in my old job. I felt as if I was being 'Buried Alive in the Blues', as Janis Joplin so ably puts it.

Amazingly, I managed to make it through to the end of the school and escaped from any reminders of the awful year I had just had by getting away from the country altogether. I knew, however, that it was not really facing up to the big issues which I neatly avoided by promising myself that the next academic year would be different.

So far so good then; By September, I'd come off my tablets, decided to give teaching one more determined effort; and, what's more, I could now actually get out of bed in the' mornings. Perfect! I wasn't necessarily happy, but then, who is? I told myself, "You just have to accept this as part of working life". Then the practice counsellor rang me up.

My GP had actually asked me if I would like to be referred in February but at that point her books were full up. To be honest, this hadn't bothered me even remotely. I was sure that I did riot need the help of a counsellor. How ridiculous and unnecessary for someone like me! I'd been on an introductory counselling course. I thought I knew all about what happened when you counselled others. So, why would I need it myself?

It was only because my partner thought I should try it that that I went for the first time and, even then, I nearly didn't go. Cynical, proud, defensive, and wary; These are the words that about sum up my attitude in our first meeting. At the end of this seemingly endless first session, however, she asked if I wanted another appointment in two weeks-time. Well, I thought, it hadn't been that bad really, so I said yes. The rest, as they say, is history, except to describe just how much how those sessions have helped me to slowly realise the source of my problems and sort them out for myself.

The outcome is that I am no longer working as a teacher. With my counsellor, I started to look at how I felt and I soon concluded that it was not the school, the staff, or the children I worked with who were at fault, but it was me who was definitely in the wrong job. What a relief! Now I feel in charge of my life again and I have returned to being the person I was and had lost sight of over the years. I have ambition. I am happy again and I have the will and determination to keep on going, even if I get knocked back along the way. For example, I am not too upset if I get rejected for a job. My relationship is back on with a real future to it. This is not to say that it is always easy, financially, or mentally. I still have days where I feel that maybe I have thrown away a good career and pension, and days where I get worried and concerned about where the money's going to come from. But these days are less frequent and less painful and, more importantly, my quality of life is much, much better.

I could have stayed where I was, but I have actively decided not to. Having the mental strength to change where you are in life takes a lot of effort. I didn't feel up to it last September even despite thinking I was back to 'normal'. I now know there is no magic normal. If you are depressed, you think sadness and hopelessness are normal.

In the words of Depression Alliance (the leading UK charity for people with depression), 'Depression is a feeling of persistent sadness involving feelings of helplessness and hopelessness. It involves not only mood but also feelings of being physically ill and of not being able to think clearly. It is one of the most common conditions in the UK affecting at least one in five people during their Lifetime. It is also one of the most misunderstood'.

I think my story shows how that misunderstanding often starts with the sufferer themselves. You do not have to live, feeling as I did, if you are prepared to admit that these feelings are not the norm. My GP's practice was luckily able to offer specialist help. If you do nothing else from reading my story, and you feel that you have my sort of problem the advice I would offer is:

Take a look at the Internet site; www.depressionalliance.org. It should help you to a fuller awareness of why you are feeling this way. Try counselling if you can, it really helped me and it will help you and, finally, try to find time for yourself and read some poetry!

The Road Not Taken

Two roads diverged in a yellow wood
And sorry I could not travel both
And be one traveller, long I stood
And looked down one as far as I could
To where it bent in the undergrowth

Then took the other, just as fair,
And having perhaps the better claim.
Because it was grassy and wanted wear
Though as for that, the passing there
Had worn them both about the same.

And both that morning equally lay
In leaves no step had trodden back
Oh, I kept the first for another day!
Yet knowing how many leads on to way,
I doubted if I should ever come back

I shall be telling this with a sigh
Somewhere ages and ages hence:
Two roads diverged in a wood and I -
I took the one 1ess travelled by,
And that has made all the difference.

Robert Frost

Don't Ever Give Up

I didn't have what might be considered a 'normal' childhood. When I wasn't at school, most of my time was spent visiting my mother in various hospital wards. Looking back on it now, I guess that's why I grew up without any friends outside of school hours. My mum passed away when I was nine, and though I'm ashamed to admit it, I don't even remember what she looked like now. Of course, that doesn't mean I don't recognise her in photographs; just that my mind's images of her are taken purely from print rather than real memory.

Memories are strange things too. Things that stand out from back then are silly, simple things. Things like the last family holiday we spent together. It was shortly after mum completed a course of chemotherapy. Determined to live life as fully as possible, she donned a wig and we set off to an amusement park on the seafront. We boarded a fast-moving ride that created lots of wind, which promptly blew the wig across the park. Rather than get upset, she just laughed it off and vowed not to wear another wig ever again.

After the funeral, I returned to complete my final year in primary school before moving on to a middle school in a different village. The first two years were pretty much ok other than taunts and jibes from other pupils because of the old-fashioned clothing and knee-length socks my dad thought it fitting for me to wear. However, by the time I was twelve, my dad had a new girlfriend who had just given birth to a baby boy. I still don't know to this day if he is my half-brother, or if he has the same father as her three older kids, and although my dad treats him like his own son, even he doesn't know for certain.

From being an only child living happily with my father in a large 3-bed semi, suddenly I had a new family and was sharing my room with three girls in two sets of bunks, while the baby boy had his own room. The cat was thrown out and went to live a few doors away where at least she could have some peace from the screaming brats that now lived with us. I was made to feel unwelcome in my own home, and since I had no desire to socialise with my 'new family', I spent a great deal of time in the kitchen with the dog. Tammy wasn't just my dog; At that time, she was my best, and probably only, friend. It wasn't to be for much longer. The second of the four kids was scared of dogs, so after the tiniest excuse they could muster, Tammy was to have her last walk to the vet. The only friend I'd had for a long time was now gone and I felt totally alone and isolated. It has since transpired that the child with the fear of dogs now shares a home with two, one of which is hers! I now know that the real reason for Tammy's demise was Kathleen's jealousy towards everything that could possibly remind dad of my mother. This included everything from furniture to the pets, and finally me!

Up until sixteen, I lived through what can only be described as some form of hell. At high school, I made some new friends, but all of them lived too far away for me to see them out of school, so I was still very much alone. My dress sense was still dictated by my father who seemed to think I should look as young and childlike as possible – probably because mum was only fifteen when she fell pregnant with me, and he was trying to be sure the same thing wouldn't happen to me. If he'd understood me at all, he would have seen there was nothing for him to worry about. I became an adult when my mum died. I had to. Someone had to do the cooking and ironing etc. while dad worked. Because of this, I was much more mature than anyone realised.

Throughout high school, I was picked on both at school, and at home. My only solace was visiting my gran at the weekends, and even there I was witness to some very ugly scenes when my grandfather would get into one of his moods and beat my gran. I have even seen him knock her to the ground then stamp on her neck shouting "Die you b*****d, die!", I think I was fourteen at the time and certainly too scrawny to take him on, though as I got older and more physically able, I promised he would never do anything like that again. Thankfully, he never did.

I've had many sleepless nights when the eldest stepdaughter, who was only three months my junior, would sadistically remove all my bedding so that I had to sleep on a bare mattress with nothing to keep me warm. Her younger sisters were terrified of her, so they would say nothing until she was asleep. The youngest girl would then tell me where the bedding was hidden. If I said anything to the 'adults' of the house about any of the goings on, I would simply be told that it was just 'a bit of fun'. It certainly was no fun for me! Neither was it fun to see dad trying to commit suicide after a huge argument with 'Beelzebub', nor when he smashed up the kitchen then laid on his stomach on the floor like a spoilt brat banging his fists and telling me if I went out of the house, he would kill himself.

I remember being taken to a child psychologist to see what my problem was and why I didn't talk much at home. Hell! It really takes a genius to work that one out! At the time, it seemed that every adult except my gran was against me, as if they were all ganging up on me, so I chose not to trust the psychologist. I didn't know she was there to help me, or that she was on my side, so I kept quiet and insisted that nothing was wrong. Finally, they gave up on me and left it at that. I got my head into my books and got through the GCSEs the best way I could. Miraculously, I managed to get good results in six of them and decided to go on and try A-levels.

As if my clothing wasn't bad enough, dad made me stay in uniform in the sixth form when everyone else was in jeans. Trying to fit in and stop all the bullying, I would sneak a pair of jeans into my bag and change in the toilets as soon as I got to school. However, the two eldest brats were in the fourth and fifth years at the same school and took great delight in making sure dad knew what I was doing. Dad's form of punishment for anything I did wrong was to hit me. I have lost count of the beatings I had from him back then. I've been thrown against a wall, thumped, picked up by the scruff of the neck and shaken, and have even had my head slammed between a door and wall then thrown onto a bed, where my dad was about to knock hell out of me, when I brought my knees up to protect myself and managed to accidentally knee him in the nuts! He thought I did it on purpose and beat me even more.

I only managed a few weeks of my A-levels, then I decided I couldn't live at home any longer. I had an early morning news round so one morning I slipped some jeans into my paper bag and set off to do my round. When I was done, I sneaked round the back of the village library and changed into my jeans, then with paper bag still on my shoulder I walked all the way to my gran's house. I arrived at 7am and I remember she had just got up. My gran knew what I'd been going through and was happy for me to stay with her, but we had to find out if it was legal. She phoned home to tell them where I was, and we made an appointment to see the education officer who gave us some advice. At the end of the week, my father arrived and took me home. Things were even worse. Now I had constant taunting from the brats about me running away. The house was so uncomfortable, I couldn't stand to be in it when my father was out, and so, on the Monday evening after school, I went to sit on the roof of a small outbuilding by the library. From there, I could watch for dad walking by on his way home from work and then walk home with him. My plan didn't work. I must've fallen asleep on the roof and when I noticed the time was long after dad finished his shift, I realised I better go home. I climbed down from the roof and started to make my way along the main road.

Suddenly, a horn blared, and a car screeched to a halt at the opposite side of the road. It was my granddad. He yelled at me to get in then took me to my gran. Apparently, they all thought I'd run away again but, of course, I was nowhere to be found. Dad and granddad had a slanging match on the street. My grandfather told my father he didn't know how to raise a child and that he was an unworthy father, dad told him he would never see me again etc. We saw the education officer again who informed us that my father could not force me to go home, but since I was not yet eighteen and therefore not a legal adult, my grandparents would have to sign as my guardians. They did so without hesitation. From then on, my life began to take a better course. I had to quit school and a part time job because they were both too far away for me to walk or cycle, and the buses didn't run early enough for them to be of any use to me. I found work in a textile mill full time. It was shifts, but I didn't mind that. Oddly, I had always said as a child that I wanted to work at this particular mill because my mother had worked there too. I bought a moped to make travelling easier and for a while I was doing well. I made new friends at the mill, but again, none of them lived anywhere near me and all had their own set of friends away from work. We did have quite a lot of gatherings though, where we would all head to the next town and get drunk. It didn't stop at alcohol though. Quite a few were smoking all kinds of things other than tobacco and, trying to fit in, so did I. It never made me feel any different so I never actually bought any, but if one of the others handed me a 'spliff', I would accept it. At seventeen, I had a busy life. I was working full time, had a second job as a barmaid at weekends, and if I wasn't working the bar, I would be out with my workmates getting drunk.

The pub was the beginning of another problem. Actually it was not the pub, but the landlord, that was the problem. He couldn't keep his hands to himself and would grope me at every opportunity. I was young, shy, and naive at that time. I wouldn't dare tell him 'no' for fear of losing my job. I still shudder now when I think of some of the things he did. The things that I let him do! For many years I was disgusted with myself for letting it happen but, since counselling, I have come to realise he was the one in the wrong, not me. Matters were made worse because his long-term partner was my closest friend at the time. We shared a love of horses and riding which formed the basis of a good friendship. Because of that, I not only felt dirty and frightened, but also guilty. For all the heartache the landlord caused me, I did love my job and I didn't want to lose it. I met my current partner while I was working there, and I knew all the customers well, but I could only take so much. One night after the customers had all left, I was in the kitchens washing the ashtrays when the landlord walked in. He was about to take hold of me when I told him I wasn't going to take it anymore. He looked shocked, but then his expression turned to one of anger. He told me; "I'll make your life very difficult." I told him to find some new bar staff and walked out. I think that was the start of the new 'tougher' me.

In any case, I was getting bored with all the constant pubs, clubs, and nightclubs so I would make excuses not to go out. I was more mature than most of my colleagues even though I was the youngest. I didn't enjoy partying like them. I preferred a quiet drink and a game of pool. Another friend would always make some excuses too. She told me that when she was out with the others, they acted so childishly that she felt like she was their grandmother. That was how I felt too, so although I remained friendly with the crowd during working hours, I began to socialise with them much less. I was also tiring of shift work. I wanted a job with normal daytime hours. I made my feelings known to the management who offered me a daytime position in one of the offices. I took it but it wasn't for me. Far too often there was nothing to do but sit and wait so I went back to the mules and the shifts.

On my return to the mule shed, I noticed some peoples' attitudes towards me had changed. It was as though they presumed that I felt 'above' them just because I had been in a different part of the building, and they resented it. At lunchtime, some would sit in the canteen, some by the dam, and some would sit on the floor in the mule shed with feet dangling out of the loading bay doors. I was one of the latter. One day, after we had eaten, we rolled some yarn into a ball and were playing around with it in the doorway. It went straight through the opening and down to the driveway below us. We couldn't just leave it. If the bosses had seen it, they would have gone mad, so I went to retrieve it. Just as I was extending my arm to pick it up one of my so-called friends spat on me. I returned with the yarn and punched her only to be asked "What was that for?".

From then on, I was more determined than ever to find a new job and within the week I had an interview. It was still a mill, but it was a regular day shift and I loved it. There was a friendly atmosphere all round, not just the workforce, but the management and owners were also very amiable. I stayed there for four years but had to leave because the business had started to sink. We were working short time on a regular basis, and I couldn't afford it, so I left and went to work at yet another mill near to my home.

Shortly after starting my third job, I began to experience problems with my health. Although they never admitted it, I know that most people at work didn't believe me. That's ok, my doctor at the time didn't believe me either! If she didn't think I was ill, then how could I expect my employers to take me seriously? In the end, one locum GP did take me seriously. He arranged for me to see a specialist who began numerous tests, but nothing showed up. After several non-productive visits to both the hospital and my own GP, I decided to change to another practice. As luck would have it, the locum who had been helpful to me earlier would turn out to work there and is now my full time GP. At last, I had someone who really believed that I was (and still am) ill. It was a shame that my boyfriend and many of my family members didn't feel that way too. They were convinced that I was either putting it on, or exaggerating, or that it was all in my head. My boss was also among the group of non-believers. He didn't sack me outright because, to my knowledge, that's illegal whilst the employee is on the sick. Instead, he made me redundant. There wasn't much I could do about it, I had only worked there for about 18 months, so I had little, if any, rights. Although I was gutted at the time, I now know that he did me a huge favour.

Since then, I have been diagnosed with ME/CFS (myalgic encephalomyelitis/chronic fatigue syndrome). I can't begin to describe what a relief it was to finally have a diagnosis; to finally know that I was right, that I am ill, that all those cretins who doubted me were wrong! That's why my last boss did me a favour by "making me redundant" – the best treatment for ME/CFS is rest, rest, and more rest. At least now I no longer had a job, I didn't have to drag myself to my machines every day and consequently make myself even more ill.

At this point, my GP recommended that I seek counselling. I couldn't see what help that would be, but I agreed to try anything. That was about 18 months ago. The counselling, although it can't physically help, has made me feel so much better about myself. I still do have problems aplenty, but with the help and support of the group I now attend, I feel more equipped to cope. I have more focus; I know what I want to do with my life and I have taken steps to achieve my goals. It's hard going because of the constant setbacks, but with the support of my counsellor, and of the wonderful people who make up the group, I know I'll get there in the end.

So, what are my current problems? Well, my health is still a major factor. Whilst I am still suffering the effects of ME/CFS, I can't look for another job. I am much better than I was two, three, four years ago, but by no means well yet. I'm determined that I will recover fully, no matter how long it takes. I am using some of the time I now spend at home to study towards a new rewarding career in IT, and I'm hoping that the qualifications I am aiming for will help me to get a green card (work visa) to move to the US. I have wanted to move there for quite a while. They have a better standard of living, better pay, and as part of the symptoms of my illness, I don't live and sleep the usual UK hours. My internal body clock is western – that is what the CFS clinic told me, though I already knew that. My sleeping pattern is EST (New York) so as many people here are just beginning their day at 5am, I am just retiring to bed. For me it is midnight. I hope that moving stateside will eliminate that, and help to control, if not eradicate, many of my symptoms.

Moving to America would also greatly improve my happiness. I'm not at all happy in my current arrangement.

Why should I want to move to America? Well, I met an American guy living in the area. We got on really well and became lovers. This went on for a few months until he told me that he was married. I must confess that I wasn't really surprised at this and still felt a great deal about him. We talked about things, and he decided that maybe we should take a break while he tried to make a go of it with his wife.

Thinking it was just cold feet, and that we could forget about each other, I encouraged him to go on with it. I thought it was the right thing to do, that I would get over him and move on, that he too would forget about me and be happy with his new wife. I couldn't have been more wrong. His wife shows him very little love or affection and he now seriously regrets the marriage. He wants to end it, but he is scared of being alone, and also scared that his family may see him as a failure. I'm not going into detail here because that is his business, and there are things that he has confided in me that I will take to my grave. What I will say is that we both firmly believe that we are soulmates, and many of our friends who know about our relationship also think that it is "meant to be". His beliefs are totally different to those of his wife, and what little time they do spend together, they spend fighting.

He wants me to move to the US to be with him, I want that too. His family already knows that his marriage is on the edge, and his friends, colleagues, and some family members know about me. He has recently been looking into divorcing his wife so that he can marry me, and hence I get my green card. Better than that, I get permanent residency. I love him with all my heart and soul, and he has told me he loves and needs me.

So, here's my dilemma: My family don't know about my American lover, or even of my desire to emigrate. They use emotional blackmail to force me to stay with my current partner, even though I have tried to leave him on a few occasions. They put on the 'water-works' whenever I try to leave. It makes me feel guilty. My current partner turns up begging me to go back, telling me he'll change, he'll do anything and so on. So, I go back. Things are ok for a short while, but then it's back to the same bad old ways. I am just biding my time, taking comfort in my American dream.

Something snaps, the last straw – again! This time, I leave while my gran is in hospital having a breast operation. Bad timing, I know, but at least I got a couple of days of peace. When she gets out of hospital, she tells me I am making her more ill etc. Of course, I've heard it all before but what can I do? Yet again my partner begs me to come home. This time he promises to sell his house and buy a smaller one in joint names and use the excess money to eradicate all our debts. I don't want to go home, but between his pleas, and my grandmother's emotional blackmail (maybe that's not what she intends, but it's certainly what it feels like to me), I agree to try one more time.

Currently, I am back with my partner and all his promises. Not that he has acted on any of what he has said yet. I'm not happy and I still want to emigrate. I'm not in a position to emigrate or get my own place here because of financial reasons. So, what do I do now? What would you do?

Ok, concentrate! Here's the serious bit! What have I learned? What has all this taught me? Hmmm, tough one! Well, it's taught me never to give up on my dreams. Since beginning my counselling, I've been able to come to terms with most of what life has thrown at me. What is really strange is that before I started, I didn't think that any of it was still locked away inside in the first place. I wasn't referred for counselling so much for depression and anxiety, as I was for a "we'll try anything just in case" approach when all medical tests were drawing a blank as to what was wrong with me.

Initially, I couldn't see how talking to someone would help anything. I was so very wrong, it does help, it helps to make sense of everything, it helps put things in perspective, it has helped, and is still helping, me to become stronger, more confident, more determined to make the most of my life. I have been able to realise my own strengths and weaknesses, and I am still learning. At first relationship, yet because I can't work, I am trapped. I can't support myself financially so I can't get my own place. I can't stay with family members because the only one who has a spare room can't accommodate my dog as well as me. My dog is my child in many ways, and just as you would never ask a parent to leave his/her child behind, I won't leave my dog. When I go to the US, he will travel with me.

I have just been to see my bank manager who has agreed consolidation of all my debts into a payment that

I can afford with ease. This is a huge relief for me and a massive weight off my shoulders. I had enough left over to set myself up in business, the proceeds of which, I hope, will enable me to buy a business in the US to be eligible for permanent residency. Things are looking up for me again. This is why I say never give up!

The heart must have its autumn, its pale skies heading, mayhap, to winter's dim dismay. Yet doubt not, beauty doth not pass away. Secure beneath the earth the snowdrop lies waiting the spring's young resurrection day. Through the kind nurture of the winter's cold, thy sorrow is the husk that doth enfold a gorgeous June.

George MacDonald.

Being Myself

I am seventeen years old, and it all started when I was ten years old and left junior school for high school. I was one of the youngest and I was really keen to start high school and to have my eleventh birthday in the holiday. My birthday finally came, and I couldn't wait till the second of September and starting my new school. When it came, I thought I would be in my element but the moment I sat down I knew I didn't fit in with anyone. Even on the first day, I got called names, but I just brushed it off thinking not everyone can be so cruel and, surely, I don't look too much like my sister who I knew was also bullied at school. I tried to be discreet for the first year and I suppose it worked, just speaking to the few friends I had. But halfway through the second year was where the bullying started. I was twelve and a half and, as most people know, your body changes in different ways when you start to grow, I was putting on weight left, right and centre.

It was bad enough me knowing I had a weight problem, let alone anyone else making a thing of it and, on top of that, my emotions changed when I hit puberty. When I was in my third year and I was aged thirteen, I couldn't even walk down a corridor without having something shouted at me. I even had the first-year pupils calling me names, and I couldn't do a thing about it. Sometimes, I could have killed them if I could have got my hands on them and that is how I felt. I knew there was something wrong with this, but they were just copying the older ones. They made me feel so small, like I didn't exist. After a while, I started to smoke and we used to go to someone's garden, I hung around with mostly boys because in my short experience girls can be evil.

One day, I was in my lesson and a girl I knew asked me if I was coming for a smoke, so as we walked down, I looked into the entrance and two girls grabbed hold of me and pulled me in. One punched me in my head five or six times then the other grabbed me and kneed me in the face and swung my head into a tree. As I was trying to get free, one of the lads grabbed me to try and restrain me. The worst thing was he was related to me. When I did get free, I ran so fast that all I could think about was that there was about twenty people in that entrance and not one of them tried to help me. My mum phoned the police and later that night I had to go to hospital with concussion.

The girls got away with attacking me and after that I hardly went to school and tried slashing my wrists. I was so down that my doctor put me on anti-depressants. I was 13 and I felt like a freak taking pills so, in the end, I just came off them. In the 4th year I started to drink with the homeless people in town; Cider, of all drinks. I knew it was wrong but these folk made me feel wanted. Most days, I would have spent my dinner money on a bottle of cider and there were a lot of other young ones messing around either skiving off an odd lesson or two or not even bothering go to school at all. Some of them were from broken homes or didn't have family so we all talked about our problems. One day, I had one too many drinks and I was lying on the floor throwing up all that I had drunk. I couldn't lift my head at this point, and the other young ones had gone off for a fight, when the school social worker found me. He took me home, but all he had to say is "Why are you like this? You come from a good background, your parents are pillars of the community" (whatever that means), but all I can say is that no-one knows what happens behind closed doors, do they?

If he had been interested at all, he would have found out that my mum and dad didn't really care about me anyway. If truth be told, I thought that they thought that, as I was the one who couldn't read or write or spell, I would never amount to anything. I hated my parents at that time, but I have to admit that I did misbehave at home. That was mostly to get attention from them. I tried to explain why I didn't want to go to school, and that school wouldn't do anything about it, after all what is the point in telling everyone just for one girl anyway. I felt as if no-one would notice that I wasn't there if I just went away.

If I got to my form room without one name been called at me, it was a good day. But the thought of being alone made me cringe. Once, when I was on the bus to school, I looked down at the group of people at the gates. It was almost like they waited just for me to give me their 'welcomes' as they did all through the day when they saw me. That's why I just stayed on the school bus until it arrived in town. When I did actually go into school, it was like the crowd of other girls were robots – as if someone had programmed them to say the horrid things – mostly things about my weight – which hurt so much. When I got to the last year, I was hardly ever seen in school and when I was there, I would spend most of my time with the school nurse who was the one person who was nice to me. Finally, I did my exams and left, yes! It was over.

Things got a lot better; I was having fun going out around town to the pubs and clubs at such a young age but I had been drinking for a long time. Then one weekend I had a one-night stand with a man old enough to be my dad well, just, he was thirty-one. I don't know what possessed me to do that but, from then on, I was associating sex with love and sleeping with anyone to find the right person for me, and I mean anyone! I even had a relationship with a girl, so I was asking myself am I gay!? But as I was trying to find love they just thought of me as a slag, which I'm not! I stayed in contact with the older man but then I lost his number when I had my phone stolen at my old job about eight months before my 17th birthday.

I was then going out with a boy I met through a friend, and I got the older man's phone number (I won't give his identity away, so I'll call him Jay) and I whilst I was out with the boy in town we had an argument, which led to him leaving me in the middle of the town with no money. I rang Jay and told him what had happened. He came and picked me up in his car and took me to his house, it was really weird how it all happened so fast. I met his kids the next morning, and his mum and dad soon after that.

I was at his house every weekend, and after a month or so I wanted a proper relationship with him. Four months in I loved him, yet he didn't seem interested really. So I pushed and I pushed and the perfect opportunity came along. My mum and dad were kicking me out and I turned up on his doorstep, he couldn't really push me away under the circumstances after all I had been sleeping with him for about four or five months. As the weeks passed on, however, he hardly did anything.

He quit his job because he said he just had had enough of working, and he was in debt up to his eyeballs with maintenance and other things. I didn't see his faults because I was in love with him so much. We couldn't do anything without his mum butting her nose in every two minutes and he wouldn't stick up for himself, or for me, so I sort of knew he didn't want me there although he was still prepared to sleep with me every night.

He was always on drugs, and gradually I started smoking cannabis with him and his mates. As my 17th birthday approached, we hardly spoke but sometimes he would be so nice to me, like he would run me baths and make tea. Those were the things that made me put my thoughts of neglect to the back of my mind. The day of my birthday, I went round to my mums and when I got back, he had made me a lovely meal but he wouldn't make an effort to come with me and tell my parents he did want me and loved me.

Three weeks later, I went to London to visit my cousin and we were going to go on a day trip to Paris. By the time I got to London, however, I felt very ill. I thought it was because I had been drinking the night before. Something wasn't right, the sickness wouldn't go away but it didn't click. I was drinking heavily in London as I'd become a big drinker anyway but all week I was so ill. Then one night I told my cousin I might be pregnant. She was shocked and thought it was the bottle of whisky we had just drank and brushed it off, but as I was sleeping all the time, she got suspicious too and begged me to do a test when I got home because the slightest thing would set me off crying.

When I got home, Jay ran me a bath. I felt so happy and pushed my thoughts of Jay not loving me to the back of my head. I just knew I was pregnant, I had to be! So later on that night, I got the test from my bedside table. I had taken one a few weeks before because we never used any contraception. I'm sure he thought I was infertile or something. When I was taking the test, he was in the living room with his children and his friends and their kids. We were going to a concert in a local park, so when it showed positive, I was so happy. When I told Jay, he walked straight out of the room and just said; "Leave it for today, we will talk about it later." But that was all he said.

When I told my mum, she went mad. She was so upset that I was going to throw my life away like this but all I could think about that was that she always thought I would amount to nothing anyway so what was the point! I was so happy even though everyone else wanted me to get rid of the baby inside me. My mum and sisters were getting at me all the time and so was Jay's mum, saying I was trapping him and talking about my age. Then Jay said he didn't want it and that he couldn't cope; that he had depression! I just laughed in his face, but I was so hurt about that it sent me on a downer. When I went to the doctor's, I was seven weeks gone, she even told me when it would be due. It was going to be in May.

I was happy but no one else was. Then one morning I woke up and I jumped out of bed, I was losing a lot of blood; I mean gushing with blood. I was so scared. I rang my mum straight away and she said; "Go to the hospital, I'll meet you there." When I went in the living room, it was 6am and Jay was still up, he hadn't been to bed all night. I asked him to come up to the hospital with me and he said that he was too tired. I couldn't believe it. I went at him like a raging bull, so he got his pants and put them on, and me being mad told him not to bother. If he wasn't going to come with me because he loved me, then he should just not bother. So he got a temper on and threw the table across the room, I just got my coat and left. I couldn't believe that he had left me to go to the hospital alone, on a bus as well, but when I got there, I ended up staying in and Jay came up for about five minutes – he didn't even give me a hug. I was in for three days, he visited twice.

It was the worst three days of my life until then. I rang him one time and he said he was at home in bed. I later found out he was in the pub with a girl he knows. He didn't give a monkey's about me, so I went back home with my mum. After having a scan, the heart was still beating but there was nothing to hold on to. I was told there was only a very slim chance that I would come out with a baby. They said; "Either you'll have a miscarriage or maybe a stillborn." I had to make the hardest decision I have ever had to in my life: To give up hope of having my baby. I then found out I had an S.T.D. from Jay, which was what was causing the blood clots and the haemorrhaging. I couldn't believe it! Jay had got what he wanted, I felt like it was his fault. Well, if he had been cleaner, I wouldn't have got it from him. I made my decision and went through with a termination; It was so hard on me, and I was so down. Jay didn't have anything to do with it, my parents took me and, as much as I appreciated them for it, the only person I still wanted was Jay.

I cried for ages then, a few weeks after, my sister found out she was pregnant. Well, that hurt me even more. I hated her but I shouldn't; It was not her fault, just bad timing and like a silly, silly little girl, I went back to Jay and started sleeping with him again. I knew it was wrong but I still loved him so much. Then after about a month and a half I thought 'What the hell am I doing?' This was after he had started ignoring my phone calls and just never being home when I went up. I confronted him about it saying; "You know I love you very much and I know you don't feel the same, but do you want to be with me?" His reply was "No". So then I knew. We hugged and I left. I felt free. I think I always knew but I had to hear it from him, and I thank him for not lying to me when I asked him. I went on a downer big time, I felt so lonely; The doctor put me back on anti-depressants but, like before, I felt I could do this without them, and he introduced me to a lovely counsellor who I really enjoy talking to and feel happier after I have done.

It's now a few months on, and I am still seeing the counsellor and feeling a much better as I have learned a lot of lessons in my last few years. What I have been through is bad, but it has taught me a few things about life; How not to push on people and to take things slower. I wouldn't wish my past on anyone but as the saying goes what doesn't kill you only makes you stronger. I know now I wasn't supposed to be a mum just yet, and I have dealt with it in the best way I can. In my prayers I have asked a friend of mine, who died when I was in school, to take my baby in her arms and look after her until I can see her again.

I have grown up a lot since what happened with the baby and it has made me want to settle down; Not just with a loved one, but to think about my future in a different light and to stop acting like a baby at times. I can never forget about what I have been through and the reasons why I got into the situation I was in. I know that I won't go down that line again, but I don't regret it altogether because I have learnt from it all. I forgive the people that have hurt me in the past and don't hold a grudge. It is all part of life even though, perhaps, it shouldn't have happened. It did happen though, and I have to deal with that.

I wouldn't say that I am over it, but I am getting there. I have met someone else. Well, I have known him all my life and we are really good friends. More than anything, I love his company and he loves mine too. It is now six months on, and I am now engaged and very happy, getting ready to move out of my parent's house and start my own. If I had to give someone else advice in my situation, all I would say is you don't have to do it all alone. Try not to push people away like I did when they are only trying to help you. Go to your doctor and ask about speaking to someone for counselling because, although some people think it is a myth, talking to someone really does help and only a few very lucky people have a close friend or family to help with it. Like many in my position, I didn't have my family as such by my side because I was pushing them away by my behaviour. We just didn't get on. My goal now is to be a counsellor myself one day and to help others in my situation understand it is ok to grieve. Remember, don't try to do this on your own, there is help.

It has just gone past the date that I was meant to have my baby. That day was hard for me, but I wasn't alone and, shortly afterwards, my sister had her baby, and she is the most beautiful little girl I have ever seen. I thank my mum and dad for being there for me now and for understanding that though I did play up as a teenager, it was purely to get attention. They know that I realise I don't have to do that anymore. All I have to do is be myself.

Your children are not your children.
They are the sons and daughters of life's longing for itself.
They come through you but not from you,
And though they are with you yet they
belong not to you.
You may give them your love but not your thoughts,
For they have their own thoughts. You may house their bodies but not
their souls,
For their souls dwell in the house of tomorrow,
which you cannot visit, not even in your dreams.
You may strive to be like them, but seek not to make them like you.
For life goes not backward nor tarries with yesterday.

The Prophet Khalil Gibran

The Heart of the Matter

My problem started about three years ago, when I developed chest pains. I went to hospital and, after tests showed nothing seriously wrong, they asked if I was worried about anything. At that time, I thought I was fine. I had a new grandson to keep me occupied and I didn't think of myself as an anxious person.

About a year later, the pains recurred. At this time my husband had been out of work all year due to a knee injury and my daughter then lost a baby at twenty-seven weeks. I must admit, I found this very hard to accept. I went to see my GP again and was told that my symptoms were probably due to anxiety and panic attacks. The pains continued, however, and after one particularly bad attack I was finally admitted to hospital as an emergency with a real heart attack. I was allowed home on medication after a week, but I was very afraid that it might happen again and felt very insecure leaving hospital. This led to more anxiety, depression and panicky feelings.

When I got home, my doctor came to see me and we discussed my feelings. He thought that my daughter's loss and my own health problems were making me very depressed. I wouldn't leave the house; I couldn't concentrate to read or watch TV and my appetite disappeared. All I wanted to do was stay in bed and escape into sleep. I found it hard to talk to anyone about my feelings until the doctor suggested I saw a counsellor. It is only since then that I have been able to talk about my feelings. It helped me such a lot as did the support and encouragement I had from my family.

Counselling opened up my life again. The counsellor encouraged me to talk about all my worries and feelings. My family supported me through it all and, by gradually taking some exercise and watching my diet, it got me feeling much better. Even now, I sometimes find it hard to put my feelings into words, but I am getting much better and now feel able to express my hopes and fears more easily and to go out to work and do all the things I used to enjoy again. I now feel as if I can finally get on with my life and do all the things I never thought I would do again.

Talking through things has helped me much more than taking a load of pills. The heartache I felt was, at least, in part coming from my fears and sadness and addressing these and the action of getting my worries off my chest has literally taken a load off me and allowed me to get my life back on track.

About Talking

When you meet your friend on the roadside or in the market-place,
let the spirit in you move your lips and direct your tongue.
Let the voice within your voice speak to the ear of his ear;
For his soul will keep the truth of your heart
as the taste of the wine is remembered.
When the colour is forgotten and the vessel is no more.

The Prophet Khalil Gibran

Finding my Life

I am a faery Queen! I am here to allow natural beauty to live and natural powers to be known. I am honest and true. I am the call of the seagull, the hoot of the owl, the breeze through the birch tree, the tiny spider in the garden and I am also a human being; but, as a person, I sometimes have faced a series of deep dark tunnels and hardships.

In my life, I have been as innocent as a young child. My mind has run free, and my eyes noticed everything. My heart seems to feel everything too. Sometimes, even now as a successful and generally happy adult, I look at the Hawthorne tree full of frothy May blossoms gently moving as it overhangs the ancient stone wall and is reflected in the pool at the edge of a field of buttercups, and I simply want to merge, and become one with that vista. Not to be human anymore. Rather to be part of the huge spirit within nature. I believe that I am indeed a creature of the spirit, at one with natural beauty and with much love to give to the world.

In spite of what you might think, I am not a dreamer! My head is squarely on my shoulders and, nowadays, I am really quite pragmatic about my life as a songwriter, dancer, singer, guitarist, music teacher and painter. I have been dancing, singing and painting since I was two but never felt that I had the support that a gifted and enthusiastic young adult needed. Nevertheless, my life as an artist has been aided by my own practical mind and I could fight and survive on my own in the world. My songs and paintings come from the deep well of mystery and drama which is present in nature. The ancient Celtic faces and places speak to me, and I respond. I feel a natural affinity to rural Ireland. I fell in love with the sound of the place when, as a young child, my father first described what he saw on a business trip there. Since then, I have visited many times and find myself uniquely at home. Ireland greets me as a loving grandmother, as a beautiful maiden and as a little child. Mother Nature personified. Welcoming, caring, exuberant and giving. The warmth and happiness of the people, the freshness of the countryside and seashores, the quality of the light; All seems to fill me with energy and heal my heart and body in a way I have felt nowhere else in the world so that I am inspired to sing and write and paint.

Without my gifts, I am not sure how I would have survived. I now feel that I was thrown to the lions but came out the victor. I became the lion's friends. I tamed the lions of my own adversity, but it has taken all my life so far and every last drop of my spirit. My hopes and dreams are at last coming true. My goals in life have, I suppose, been to have a secure roof over my head, the right person to support me and time to pursue my endeavours as a musician and artist but to secure these goals has been a monumental struggle.

To start at the beginning, I was born and brought up in the North of England. Went away for three years to study, and travelled in Europe, America and Western Asia. I believe, however, that I would have had the same personality even had I been born in a different place or circumstances. I know I do not fit well into most people's idea of 'normal', a life of politics, football, soap operas, school and work. I am even removed from the idea of national identity. This doesn't bother me anymore. I am bright enough to create my own world with the people I love and admire. To get to this point took me years of slow development. The other day whilst working with another musician in my studio, he remarked on how my compositions seemed to have a continuity and connection. One grows out of another. I know that my paintings represent the connections I feel to exist between the many different worlds we inhabit, animal and plant, sea and sky, reality and spirit, with the placement of vulnerable humanity between.

For the first two decades of my life, I searched for spiritual meaning. I closely examined all religions but eventually came back full circle to Mother Nature and the beauty of the natural spirit. Really all that there is, is the One Great Spirit encompassing love at its heart. I feel that the real truth is out there with the mountains, sea and sky and with the birds, animals, trees and flowers. They speak to the artist of the real and deeper spiritual nature of our world. Faced with the loving spirit of nature what we perceive as bad things are really pitifully small. The creative force of the universe is positive and easily overcomes the negative forces of evil or else our universe would have disappeared billions of years ago.

I do think a lot about the workings of life and nature. I love being at one with my natural surroundings. This is so much a part of life that I find it difficult to switch off and go on holiday or even a day trip without taking my paints and guitar. I feel much happier and mentally balanced when I am being creative. I feel most happy when I am in the middle of composing or painting. When these go well then I am really happy and contented, but there were times when I didn't know that great spirit. The

God I was taught to salute as a child just didn't seem real to me; but how was I to find the real One? I can see deep, eternal things buried in nature. There is, for example, a well-known mathematical symmetry algorithm called the Fibonacci number, which is given as the ratio of 1.62, and which underlines our perception of what is beautiful to look at.

I have had to break away from all the people who tied me up and free myself to be who I truly am and develop as an artist. To develop this degree of self-confidence has been difficult but once I realised I had skills and ability, my life changed. Sadly, my parents and family gave me no self-esteem along the way. They never offered favourable comments nor praised me to those around. I had a tough start to life in that way. I had to develop my own self esteem to survive and, in this, my most dangerous opponent was myself! With a happier childhood, and more positive love and affection, I would never have had so much self-doubt and unhappiness through my childhood, and adolescence up to my early thirties. I worried that by allowing myself any happiness I would lose self-control of my life. I used self-control to regulate and determine my happiness.

I now see that my few fears come from past events whilst my dreams and hopes are in the future. By allowing myself to live my life as I want it to be, it has become more right for me. This was not a philosophy encouraged by those who brought me up and wished me to emulate their lives. Their ideas were often forced on me both verbally and, at times, physically. Their views were those of bigoted and closed minds. They shunned any kind of unorthodoxy and were racist, sexist, ageist and even size-ist! They believed that it is the male who is the identity of humankind and that the females were only there as handmaidens and helpers. They never connected with anyone of different race, faith or ideology. When, as a 25year old I took my dear Malaysian friend, Sudyan, to visit my parents, they quickly disappeared into another room and refused to speak to Sudyan or, indeed, with me for the whole evening. I was hugely embarrassed and devastated that they could behave in this way to my friend.

My family favoured white, male, successful people with high incomes, nice cars, well behaved children, nice dogs (no cats please!) taking nice holidays to nice places where you could have a laugh about the natives when you got home. They were very suspicious of arty folk, businesswomen, lefty schoolteachers, university academics, men with long hair, single working women, the clergy and people with seemingly exceptional ability unless at a safe distance such as on the television! They idealised rich businessmen with profitable firms, Mercedes, powerboats in the Lakes. It appeared to me that to achieve their gains these same men seemed to have such stressed out existences, fuelled by G&T afternoons and heavy lunches, that they had no time for any cultural life. Most of those my parents knew seemed to burn out quickly and die before they made retirement age!

Of all the people my family shunned, however, I soon realised that I was top of the list. They had nothing but praise for their friend's children. Their conversation with me would run like this: "Oh! Janet is learning to type, how clever!", or "James and Katherine are getting top marks at school – they'll end up in good jobs, I'm certain!". I knew that I incorporated so many of the people they hated that I was more contemptible that any artist, teacher, lecturer, vicar or hippy – and they made sure I knew it. Although I was a busy teenager, I had no desire to go down the conformist road.

When I was eleven, I followed my brother to a private tutor for extra help in the main subjects. In this time, I actually sat and passed past GCE exam papers in maths. Once he had taken his GCE exams though, my parents didn't feel I was worth the extra cost and my extra tuition stopped. By the age of 14, my parents and teachers decided that as I was of merely average ability and that I would not study for 'O' levels as I hadn't the aptitude. Instead, at the age of fifteen, I left school with ten C.S.E.s most of which were a respectable grade 2.

By the age of eighteen, I had managed to catch up and then got a good degree. A while ago, I actually took a MENSA test which showed that I have a very high IQ. How could my parent's view of me be so wrong? To this day, their assertion has been that my view of the world was wrong, and their view of life was the only real world which was proven by their success, holidays, cars, boats and income. They did not believe that anyone like me, who had to save up for a new pair of shoes and couldn't afford to buy a house or a car, could possibly have it right. When I first acquired the MENSA test papers, they poured so much scorn on my even thinking of trying that I put the test in a drawer where it remained, untaken, for another four years. When I finally took it and got my results back, I chose not to tell them. By then we had parted ways and, in any case, they would probably refuse to believe that their daughter was actually very intelligent as they would have had to admit that their actions towards me based on them deciding I was worthless had always been wrong. In general, my parents, especially my mother, have been horrible to me. I have never felt love or acceptance of who I am. They have done everything to lower my self-esteem in spite of which, somehow, I have still succeeded.

"So ok," my mother said to me when I was ill in bed at the age of twenty-two; "You've managed to sell a couple of paintings for a few thousand pounds and children and animals love you – but that's not real success, is it? – we gave up on you years ago." My parents had no sympathy with anyone who was ill.

In fact, my father was basically a sweet and kind man, but he was always heavily influenced and dominated by my mother. They met as teenagers and married quite early when my dad was twenty-three and my mum twenty-one and, although the younger, she dominated the marriage so that, gradually, my father grew to be like her and took on her way of thinking and acting. As I grew up, he kept very much in the background. As I reached puberty, we became even more distanced from each other. My mother would jealously ensure we were kept apart. Very occasionally, he would stand up to her screaming demands and on rare occasions, even tell me the odd half secret about her which I had to promise never to divulge.

It wasn't all bad of course. In fact, sometimes life was good, and I remember having very happy times when, at fourteen, I joined a small modelling agency and charm school. Here I met adults who actually found something in me to praise. They taught me how to speak and walk properly and communicate clearly. I learned how to make myself look stunning and feel good about myself. School seemed irrelevant apart from socialising and showing off my clothes. I discovered I had style and a flair for fashion. My confidence with strangers grew tremendously but, of course, it had little effect on my family. I, however, felt that I was leaving them behind. I had found myself at last.

Today my hopes and dreams are many. I hope, above all, that my hard work in song writing and painting will eventually pay off by allowing me a better standard of living. I am sure that I am just as talented as some pretty famous song writers and artists. I just need a few breakthroughs to turn my living standards around. I am always a little cautious of dreams and fantasies. I try to plan things rather than dream about them, but I would really like to sing on stage in front of a good audience. I think my voice is quite unique and this has been remarked on by others. I would like a good manager and promoter to help in this, and I would dearly like to have a proper exhibition of my artwork in Galway or Dublin where many of my landscapes are based. I would like to see a return to a simpler way of life, much less influenced by big commercial concerns, where people work locally and have a less money driven lifestyle. I would like to see society return to ancient tribal values with a sense of belonging to a community and responsibility to one another whilst honouring those with gifts to offer.

So, most of my adult life was spent in fear. I was frightened of bumping into my mother or one of her horrible friends. I was frightened of failing my degree course. I was frightened of rejection in my artistic life. I was frightened of being penniless and of being totally lonely but, with help, I now find that I no longer have any real fears. I know that I am fine as me, in my own self. I have found out that I can make a life for myself and be responsible for it and allow myself to add and subtract parts of me and develop slowly as I feel I should. This leads me on to consider my feelings about things.

I have always been brim-full of feeling. Rather too much for my own good at times as I have often dwelt too long in a state of sadness about things I could not do much about. However, as I always try to think carefully before I act, I have rarely felt bad about any of my own actions. I feel that I share an instinctive understanding of nature and of animals whom I seem to be able to communicate with at an instinctive level. Similarly, I seem able to deal easily with young children and teenagers. We can communicate on an unspoken level.

I struggle with city life where nature shrinks into second place. All the hustle and bustle, the mechanised turmoil and electronic domination of the computer screen are not for me. I know that I am part of nature and that all things are connected. We know that for one tiny electron to change its state the natural laws of physics make every other atom in the whole of creation respond and adjust. A baby's smile connects to a distant star. A cloud is connected to a train, a buttercup to an ocean. My actions in life and even my decay in death leave an indelible imprint on the universe. I believe that the spirit is part of the unchangeable energy of nature and the universe.

All these parts of my life, the beliefs I hold and the way I feel about life, have brought me to where I am now.

I need to be loved. I have a wonderful and loving husband who understands and supports me in all I do. Because my own mother let me down, I crave love from my husband's mother with whom I feel a natural affinity. She is compassionate and caring and I need all the love she can give to help to fill the black hole left by my own real mother who regularly told me that I was mad and not what she expected when she planned to have a carbon copy daughter! I need to be loved by my few friends. I do not form close friendships easily. Perhaps northern folk are reserved and taciturn in their day-to-day interactions.

For some thirty-seven years, my own family had kept on making me think that they were right, and I was wrong. My mother's visits and angry lectures left me feeling that for the following week I couldn't breathe, and I became subject to numerous minor ailments. When I was at my lowest ebb a few years ago with a deep and destructive depression, my GP suggested that I saw the practice counsellor to help me sort my feelings out. I had married the love of my life but without the blessing of my family who had simply cut me off. Because I felt that I wanted to sort my life out properly, I later made the effort and telephoned to try and tell my mother that I really did love her and wanted her to love and understand me. Initially, I had to leave a message on their answerphone after which she eventually rang me back. The conversation was awkward. She said that it had been a long time. I told her of my sadness and my decision to see a counsellor and asked if she and my father would consider coming with me to some of the sessions as I felt that we all needed to engage in the process to sort things out. Initially, to my amazement, she agreed – even though I wondered if she thought it would be another platform for her to describe her disappointment in me. A few days later, however, I returned home from teaching to find she had left an abrupt message on my answerphone saying that if I thought that I needed to see a counsellor to be able to talk to them then I was, indeed, ‘off my trolley’ and as a result they would never contact me again! That was in 1997 and since then I have had hardly any contact with all the thirty remaining members of my own family.

Counselling helped me to gain confidence in what I was doing and know that, whatever my family thought, this was right for me. It allowed me to develop my singing voice and turn myself around. The process was a bit scary. The answers came from inside me and what if I was wrong? After all my father’s view was that all artists were parasites. Would becoming an artist turn me into a parasite living off others?

The key to freeing myself from this mental bondage lay within me, and in learning to define myself and my family in my own words. It is as if I was born on a large military aeroplane which contained all my family and was run with a successful but very strict code of discipline and social structure. The plane was spacious and most of the occupants were happy to stay in this craft and conform to the code. My father was the pilot and my mother supreme commander whose orders could not be disobeyed. I quickly found out that I didn’t fit in with the others on board and after living a miserable life for many years I decided to jump out even though I was uncertain whether or not I had a parachute. After an initially gut-wrenching fall where I questioned my sanity in jumping, I began to realise that I could dream up my own parachute. Small at first, it gradually grew, became more and more colourful and, eventually, not only supported me with its brilliant colours but allowed me to steer it and float around at my own speed. At last, I was in control of my own life and could trust my own judgement and, what is even better, for a few brief moments in that journey, I felt that I experienced the intense light of the Great Spirit. I do not say that I felt this in a particularly religious sense but take it as an understanding that there is more than we can ever know. I can sense the beauty in the souls of those I meet, both human and animal, and the experience the essence of the universe and I try to reflect this into my work.

So where am I now? I feel that I am a human who lives close to the Great Spirit in nature. I do not fear life or death. I want to achieve all that I am capable of and now that I have found that I am comfortable with my own life I am looking forward to the rest of my life's journey.

You are what your deep, driving desire is.
As your desire is, so is your will.
As your will is, so is your deed.
As your deed is, so is your destiny.

Verse translated from Sanskrit in the Brihadaranyaka Upanishad

The Glue of Life

The glue of life;
A sap so thick,
Slowly
dripping
down
the
tree,
Catches and engulfs all
But the most resourceful and the quick.
Covering and drowning what might be
Within its sticky, crystal wall.
To be sure, it preserves the status-quo;
The daily to and fro -
Maintained, and trapped
Within its oozing flow.
…But…
Still then lies the life that never was.
Stopped forever in its tracks, because,
To keep us ever as we are,
It only lets us get so far.
Just the few fly high and do not stick,
Whilst most, forever, are walled up,
Their wildest dreams made amber brick.

John Clayden, 2014.

Criteria for Counsellors

The Counsellor should preferably be a member of the British Association for Counselling (BAC) and thereby work within a recognised code of professional conduct and ethics.

The Counsellor should be covered by vicarious liability insurance whilst working for a practice. If counsellors are self-employed they must have adequate professional and public liability insurance.

An appropriate job description needed to be written for the post of Practice Counsellor. Confidentiality clauses should be stressed in any contract.

Another appropriately trained and qualified counsellor should be identified to provide a 'safety net' service in the event of unavoidable long-term absence of the acting Practice Counsellor, in accordance with the BAC Code of Ethics.

Bibliography

1) Corney, R. & Jenkins, R., *Counselling in General Practice* (1993) Ch.1. Routledge 858-859.

2) Ellenberger, H.F., *The Diversity of the Unconscious: The History and Evolution of Dynamic Psychiatry* (1970) London Allen Lane.

3) Mcleod, J., *Counselling in Primary Health Care, the GP's perspective*, in Sheldon, M., *RCGP Clinical series on counselling in General Practice* (1992) London RCGP enterprises.

4) Burks, H.M. & Stefflre B., *Theories of Counselling* 3rd Edn (1979) New York McGraw Hill.

5) Karasu, T.B., *The specificity against non-specificity dilemma: towards identifying therapeutic change agents* (1986) American Journal of Psychiatry 143: pp 687-95.

6) Mcleod, J., *An Introduction to Counselling* (1993) Open University Press pp 1-21.

8) Priest, R.G., Vize, C., Roberts, A., Roberts, M. and Tylee, A., *Lay people's attitudes to treatment of depression: results of opinion poll for Defeat Depression Campaign just before its launch* (1996) BMJ 313.

9) Anderson, S. & Hasler, J., *Counselling in General Practice* (1979) Journal of the RCGP 29: 352-6.

10) Waydenfield, D. & Waydenfield, S.W., *Counselling in General Practice* (1980) Journal of the RCGP 30: 671-7.

11) Marsh, G.N. & Barr J., *Marriage guidance counselling in a group practice* (1975) Journal of the RCGP 25: 73-5.

12) Sibbald, B., Addington-Hall, J., Brenneman, D. and Freeling, P., *Investigation of whether on-site general practice counsellors have an impact on psychotropic drug*

prescribing rates and costs (1996) Feb. British Journal of General Practice. 46(403): pp.63-7.

13) Cohen, J.S.H., *Marital counselling in General Practice* (1977) Proceedings of the Royal College of Medicine 70: 495-6.

14) Meacher, M., *A pilot counselling scheme with General Practitioners* (1977) Summary report, London: Mental Health Foundation.

15) Fletcher, J., Fayey, T. and McWilliam, J., *Relationship between counselling & the prescribing of antidepressants, hypnotics and anxiolytics in General Practice* (Sept 1995) British Journal of General Practice 45 (398): 467-9.

16) King, M., Broster, G., Lloyd, M. and Horder, J., *Controlled Trials in the evaluation of counselling in general practice* (May 1994) British Journal of Gerneral Practice 44 (382): 194-5.

17) Bailey, J. and Coppen, A., *A comparison between the Hamilton Rating Scale and Beck Inventory in the measurement of depression* (1976) British Journal of Psychiatry 128: 486-9.

18) Bech, P. and Rafaelsen, O. J., *The use of rating scales exemplified by a comparison of the Hamilton and Beck – Rafaelsen Melancholia Scale* (1980). Acta Psychiatrica Scandinavica Suppl. 285 128-31.

19) Bech, P., Gram, L.F., Dein, E., Jacobsen, O., Vigel, J. and Bolwig, T.G., *Quantitative Rating of Depressive States* (1975) Acta Psychiatrica Scandinavica 67: 361-70.

20) Beck, A.T., Ward, C.H, Mendleson, M., Mock, J. E. and Erbaugh, J., *An inventory for measuring depression* (1961) Archives of General Psychiatry 4: 561 - 85.

21) Beck T. A., Weissman, A., Lester, D. and Trecler, L., *The measurement of Pessimism: the hopelessness*

scale (1974) Journal of Consulting and Clinical Psychology 42: 861 - 65.

22) (H A D scale) *The Hospital Anxiety and Depression Scale* (1983) Zigmond and Snaith.

23) *Measuring Human Problems*, edited by David F. Peck and Colin M. Shapiro. Series in Clinical Psychiatry, Wiley.

24) General Practitioner Assessment Form. WYHA project on counselling in general practice.

Kirklees & Calderdale Health Authority own publication.

25) Brazier, J.E., Harper, R. Jones, M.M.B. et al., *Validating the SF36 Health Survey Questionnaire new outcome measure for Primary Care BMJ* (1992) 305: 160-64.

26) Sheppard, G., *What is Counselling* (2015) Notebook on Ethics, Legal Issues and standards for Counsellors.

Table of Contents

Versions of Life – Stories from Counselling................ 13
Introduction.. 21
Some Aims of Counselling 25
The Castle Keep 27
One Day at a Time 37
A Black Hole 49
Unwrapping Parcels 57
Changing for the better 67
The Burning of Leaves.. 75
The Wheel of Life 87
A Figure to Die For 95
Buried Alive in the Blues 133
Don't Ever Give Up 143
Being Myself.. 159
The Heart of the Matter.. 171
Finding my Life 175
Criteria for Counsellors... 191
Bibliography... 193

europe books